THE DIEHARD FOOTBALL FAN'S BUCKET LIST BLITZ

THE
DIEHARD
FOOTBALL
FAN'S
BUCKET LIST
BLITZ

101 RIVALRIES, TAILGATES, AND GRIDIRON TRADITIONS TO SEE & DO BEFORE YOU'RE SACKED

STEVE GREENBERG

Guilford, Connecticut

An imprint of Globe Pequot

Distributed by NATIONAL BOOK NETWORK

Copyright © 2017 by Steve Greenberg

Photos on p. iii © iStock.com/Daxus/homeworks255/efks

British Library Cataloguing in Publication Information available

Library of Congress Cataloging-in-Publication Data available

ISBN 978-1-4930-2823-8 (hardcover)

ISBN 978-1-4930-2824-5 (e-book)

♾™ The paper used in this publication meets the minimum requirements of American National Standard for Information Sciences—Permanence of Paper for Printed Library Materials, ANSI/NISO Z39.48-1992.

Printed in the United States of America

For Noah, the keeper of the flame.

CONTENTS

> CHAPTER VI. RITES OF PASSAGE

> CHAPTER VII. JUST DO IT

> CHAPTER VIII. I LOVE L.A.

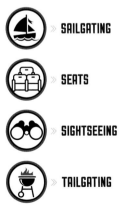

ICONS

800 CLUB	FOOTBALL MUSEUMS	SAILGATING
DIRTY DOZEN	JUST DO IT	SEATS
DOING THE SPLITS	NFL RIVALRY	SIGHTSEEING
EATS	ONE-OF-A-KIND	TAILGATING
FOOTBALL MECCAS	RITES OF PASSAGE	

» Some college football diehards from 1957.

INTRODUCTION

BASEBALL FANS connect to the sport placidly, sentimentally, but with an analytical distance. Basketball fans are enchanted with individual players. Hockey fans count the days until the Stanley Cup Playoffs. Football fans are—how to put this delicately?—insane. Every day, and all the way. Gotta love 'em. But let's call it passionate instead. Passionate about every game. Consumed with fervor for the rivalries that define the sport at every level. The rhythm of the season drives fans to the brink as they wait for Friday (high school), Saturday (college), or Sunday (NFL). The next game never fails to be the most important one, ever.

There is no such thing as a good game day or a bad game day for a football fan; game day becomes either a celebration of all that's right in the world, or an abject devastation. This—*this*—is why football rules the American sports landscape. It is intoxicating. It is utterly addictive. It's why much of this book is shaped around rivalries, the very lifeblood of the sport. Football is passion and pageantry and gladiator-strewn fields in mammoth structures set against breathtaking backdrops. Football is danger and anger and joy and relief, all to the extremes. It's the ultimate television sport, yet it can't be fully experienced without being there. So let's go there. Let's drink it in, revel in it, become filthy in it.

Ready. Set. Go. If you haven't been there already, get your bratwurst, beer, and history on at Lambeau Field, home of the Green Bay Packers. Wake up the echoes, as they say, at Notre Dame. See Ratliff Stadium in Texas, the locale of *Friday Night Lights* fame. Immerse yourself in the heated rivalries of the NFL and college football—Cowboys-Redskins, Broncos-Raiders, Ravens-Steelers, Alabama-Auburn, Michigan-Ohio State, Army-Navy. Experience the majesty of the largest venues in football, and

THE NUMBERS GAME

In 1985 pro baseball was, according to the market research firm Harris Interactive, nipping at the heels of pro football as Americans' favorite sport; 24 percent preferred the gridiron game, with 23 percent sworn to stick-and-ball. Goodness, how that has changed: In 2016 the Harris Poll determined those numbers had diverged to 33 percent and 15 percent, respectively. And guess what came in third, ahead of auto racing, men's pro basketball, and ice hockey? College football, at 10 percent. It's a football country, and we're all just living in it.

the most unique. Sit in the craziest fan sections. Stuff your face at the greatest tailgates. Marvel at the Pro Football Hall of Fame, take in the Rose Parade, cheer (and boo) at an NFL Draft, roll Toomer's Corner in Auburn, Alabama, Call the Hogs in Fayetteville, Arkansas.

But don't stop there. Spend a football weekend in a sports book in Las Vegas. Take a Gatorade shower. Step up and join the coaching staff of your kid's first football team. Look, far be it from us to suggest that you have to do all of these things. Who has the time? Who has the resources? So just try where you can. And where you can't, lean back in your favorite chair, put your feet up, and imagine being there.

A wise scribe once wrote of football: "It's not about the Xs and Os—it's about the Jimmys and Joes." True enough; it's a player's game, and we all love to watch the stars who romp into the end zone and hit like trucks. But it's about the fans, too—the people who sustain and elevate the sport. They are the Ellas and the Earls, the Lilys and the Larrys, the Bills and Phils and Wills, and so on. They are everyday folks who love football so much that it overshadows (and that's putting it nicely) every other sport in America.

So, you know: Ready. Set. Go. This here is a bucket list. And you only live once.

CHAPTER 1

MECCAS AND MUSEUMS

WHAT WRIGLEY FIELD, Madison Square Garden, Churchill Downs, St. Andrews, and the Brickyard are to other sports, these stadiums are to football. They are monuments to the game, houses of history; they are where football lives. So, too, are the archival galleries that both educate and romance visitors, that steel fans' regard for the game by bonding them with heroes past. Go. To. These. Places. And rejoice.

Football Meccas
- ► Lambeau Field
- ► Soldier Field
- ► Mercedes-Benz Superdome
- ► Notre Dame Stadium
- ► Rose Bowl Stadium
- ► Ratliff Stadium

Must-See Museums
- ► Pro Football Hall of Fame
- ► College Football Hall of Fame
- ► Canadian Football League Hall of Fame
- ► NFL Rings of Honor

In Honor of Meccas Lost to History

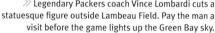

>> Legendary Packers coach Vince Lombardi cuts a statuesque figure outside Lambeau Field. Pay the man a visit before the game lights up the Green Bay sky.

LAMBEAU FIELD

IT'S BEST NOT TO ASK if more Wisconsinites know the address 1265 Lombardi Avenue than the address 1600 Pennsylvania Avenue. The answer is an easy one. No offense to fans of the Green Bay Packers, which includes every living Dairy State soul.

Lambeau Field has been home to the Packers since 1957—longer than any other stadium has housed an NFL team—and is one of the league's largest, with a capacity of over 80,000. The size of the place is a wonder juxtaposed against the challenging realities of small-market sports. Here, though, small equals hugely successful. The fans own this team, literally; more than 300,000 of them are shareholders. They are more invested—and more knowledgeable—than any other fan base, and that's indisputable.

Game days can be brutally cold, but you're not bucket-listing if you can't handle a megaton nip in the air. Hit the Packers Hall of Fame—open on football Sundays—and tailgate the right way. That means driving down one of the residential streets that surround Lambeau and finding a house with a front lawn that isn't already clogged with cars.

You'll likely be waved onto said lawn to park and be treated marvelously by a homeowner with a cooler full of beer, a grill buried in bratwurst, and a garage with a TV inside. If that sort of hospitality sets you back $25, consider yourself home.

SOLDIER FIELD

SOME CALL IT A SPACESHIP. Others call it a monstrosity. Everyone agrees it's imperfect. Yet you have to visit Chicago's Soldier Field at least once. Its setting is unlike any other—betwixt a massive downtown hubbub and the serene glory of the Lake Michigan shore—and history oozes from the place. Soldier Field has been around since 1924. The Bears have played there only since 1971, but the exterior of the building screams oldest-of-old schools. The Chicago Park District redid the place not too long ago, shoving a modern facility inside ancient walls, and that made this the oddest-looking stadium in the league. But it works in spite of itself, which captures the spirit of Chicago perfectly.

Chicago's downtown rivals that of any city, and the Bears are more important than any other local team—even the baseball Cubs—to the city's zeitgeist. When the Bears stink, the city's sports fans get drunk on bitterness. When the Bears are good, it's a season-long celebration and everyone is invited to the tailgate. Regardless, you go to Soldier Field and get the sense you're somewhere that matters, somewhere extra-heavy

≫ Soldier Field is a modern-looking facility placed inside much older, austere exterior walls with towering columns in ancient Greek style, and with brilliant views of Chicago's downtown skyline and lakefront.

with gravitas. Dick Butkus played here. Walter Payton played here. Papa Bear Halas and Mike Ditka became legends here. And it's Chicago, right? Go to the game, stay for the million and one things to do in one of the greatest cities in the world.

WHILE YOU'RE THERE

☑ Enjoy the Museum Campus in which Soldier Field sits. The Field Museum, Shedd Aquarium and Adler Planetarium are wonderful.

☑ Take a Shoreline water taxi (lake route, not river!) from Navy Pier, a must-stop for any visitor.

☑ South Loop, Printer's Row, Northerly Island, Millennium Park — so much to see and do.

>> It's still difficult to glimpse the Superdome without remembering its role in the aftermath of Hurricane Katrina. Inside, ear-splitting volume is the order of every Saints game day.

MERCEDES-BENZ SUPERDOME

LET'S BE HONEST: Part of what makes this building iconic has nothing to do with football. It regularly plays host to major national sporting events—Super Bowls, Sugar Bowls, College Football Playoff games, NCAA basketball Final Fours—because what travel-minded fan doesn't relish a visit to the Big Easy? Yet those events wouldn't continue to recur in New Orleans, particularly in football, if the Superdome weren't one of the truly great venues. The party inside rarely fails to match the party outside.

Sitting less than a mile from the French Quarter, the Superdome has been home to the NFL Saints since 1975. There are indoor venues in the NFL with more modern styling and amenities, but none where the love between fans and team is felt so palpably; also, none where it gets so loud. All this was kicked up a notch in 2005, when the Superdome hosted thousands who sought shelter from Hurricane Katrina. The love deepened, and renovations necessarily followed. The result was a building that entered a new era in better-than-ever form.

But let's hark back to the top of this write-up, because attending a game here is inextricably tied to the richness of a broader NOLA experience. If partying isn't your bag, you still have to eat, right? Hit a Saints game—or a championship game—and have a weekend you'll never forget.

≫ Do you believe in the luck of the Irish? How about in leprechauns? At Notre Dame Stadium, look to Touchdown Jesus for those and other answers.

NOTRE DAME STADIUM

KNUTE ROCKNE MAY NOT have given a stirring speech to fire up the construction crews, but the legendary Notre Dame coach was a driving force behind the creation and design of the stadium, which somehow rose from the ground to its completion in only six months. The stadium opened in 1930 for what would be Rockne's final season as coach. Notre Dame won every game that year, its fifth perfect season and third national championship under Rockne, who tragically died in a March 1931 plane crash. Irish fans will tell you the man's spirit still is felt on the home sideline, throughout the now-80,000-seat-strong stands, and all the way up to the "Touchdown Jesus" mural above the north end zone on an exterior wall of the grand Hesburgh Library.

Yet Notre Dame Stadium is more than a house of history where so many victories—and seven Heisman Trophy seasons—have unfolded. Fans in the lower parts of the bowl are as close to the field here as they are anywhere, and the sightlines are excellent no

matter where one sits. Recent massive renovations both inside and on the exterior grounds cleaned up any and all deficiencies, rendering this place better than ever. This may not be a golden era of Irish football, but games here still feel different than they do any place else. There's only one Notre Dame.

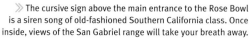

>> The cursive sign above the main entrance to the Rose Bowl is a siren song of old-fashioned Southern California class. Once inside, views of the San Gabriel range will take your breath away.

>> ROSE BOWL STADIUM

WITH THE RESURGENCE of the NFL in Los Angeles and the state-of-the-art stadium where the Rams will play, the Super Bowl and the Rose Bowl may never again intersect. It's a shame, because there is no greater football venue than the one that sits along the Arroyo Seco and gazes out at the San Gabriel Mountains. Yet it's also OK, because football—UCLA's home games, of course, as well as the sport's most iconic college bowl game—will continue to thrive there. And if not catching occasional whiffs of the NFL makes the Rose Bowl just a bit more quaint, so be it.

The Rose Bowl's landscape and beauty are so one of a kind and splendid, they truly can't be outdone. If you can get here for a Rose Bowl—the event, not the building itself—by God, do. There will be nearly 100,000 fans in the seats and echoes of great

Pac-12 and Big Ten teams all about. And talk about intersections: You'll feel like you're at the most important game ever, and in the only place worthy of such a happening. In this open-bowl stadium, there's no such thing as a bad seat. But here's a tip: Save a little dough and sit higher up—the views are better.

WHILE YOU'RE THERE

☑ **Park on the adjacent golf course grounds, which won't set you back unreasonably. You'll be nice and close, and it's a pretty place to tailgate.**

☑ **Take a hike along the dirt trail on the west side of the stadium, into the upper arroyo. You might not want to come back for the game.**

☑ **Hit the Pie 'n Burger on East California Boulevard. It's a few miles away but so worth the visit.**

RATLIFF STADIUM

BUZZ BISSINGER, AUTHOR of *Friday Night Lights*, describes the flatlands of West Texas as "where you step off into eternity and wonder if you'll ever make it back." It would be an unfair insult to the people of Odessa, Texas, to say there's nothing happening there beyond high school football. Yet the sport certainly means more there—to fans of Odessa Permian and Odessa High, both of which call Ratliff home—than it does most

>> No high school football program in our land is more storied than the Permian Panthers. When they play, life stands still in Odessa.

anywhere else. The stadium holds nearly 20,000, and it is an icon of icons. Goodness gracious, see a Permian game just so you can say you did.

HIGH SCHOOL FOOTBALL IN AMERICA, 2015– 2016 SCHOOL YEAR

>> **14,047**—high schools that fielded 11-on-11 tackle football teams

>> **1,085,272**—boys who played football at those schools, out of approximately 8 million students who participated in high school sports nationwide. Eleven-player tackle football was the top sport in terms of participation, narrowly leading outdoor track and field (1,077,102); basketball (975,808) was next, followed by soccer (821,851).

>> **1,964**—girls who played football, at 576 schools

>> **265**—schools, in four states (including 103 in South Dakota), that fielded 9-on-9 football teams

>> **834**—schools, in 17 states (including 121 in Nebraska and 111 in Kansas), that fielded 8-on-8 football teams

>> **231**—schools, in five states (including 137 in Texas), that fielded 6-on-6 football teams

>> **6.67**—high school students, out of 100, who participated in football. The all-time high was 7.4 percent, in 1989.

*Statistics courtesy of the National Federation of State High School Associations

PRO FOOTBALL HALL OF FAME

IT STARTS WITH a question: Do I want to plan my visit to the Pro Football Hall of Fame around an enshrinement ceremony? Short answer: Yes. There's nothing quite like sitting (and sweating) in Fawcett Field in Canton, Ohio, on the Saturday of the first full weekend of August as greats of the game don their Gold Jackets and speechify, with a sea of legends behind them on the dais. Ideally, you'll then stay for Sunday's Hall of Fame preseason game.

Regardless of when you visit the hall, it's an incredible place to take in. It opened in 1963 in Canton—home of the Bulldogs of the NFL-precursor American Professional Football Association—with 17 charter enshrinees; the 19,000-square-foot building contained two rooms. By 1971, the size of the place had nearly doubled and yearly attendance topped 200,000. Like the NFL itself, the hall continued to expand: to 50,000 square feet in 1978, 82,000 square feet in 1993, and eventually to 118,000 square feet. And that was before the current $500 million Hall of Fame Village development plan

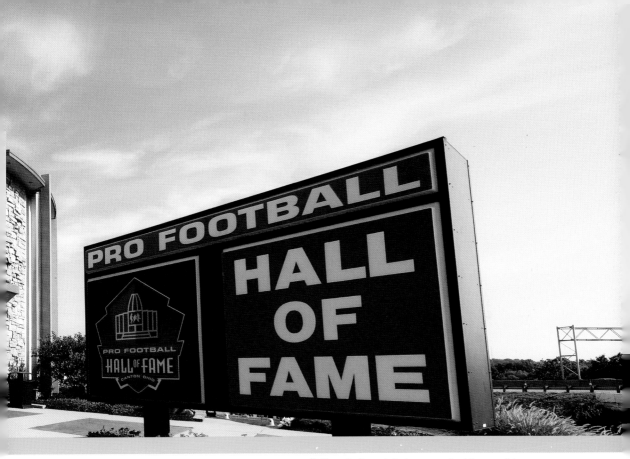

>> If you don't speak Cantonese, you're doing something wrong.
The Pro Football Hall of Fame is a must-stop for any fan.

got underway; visitors today will see incredible modern girth to the grounds, with new restaurants, shops, and a four-star hotel at which to hang one's helmet.

The Hall of Busts is, of course, the primary draw; over 300 Hall of Famers are now enshrined. Beyond the enthralling collection of artifacts and historical documents and videos are some of the best interactive options imaginable. Step into an instant-replay booth—with the same technology available to NFL officials—and make a series of calls. Throw passes to virtual receivers. Compare your body to those of NFL heroes. So much to see, learn, and do.

COLLEGE FOOTBALL HALL OF FAME

AS OF 2016, nearly 1,000 players and more than 200 coaches were enshrined in the College Football Hall of Fame. The list of players included 45 from Notre Dame, 40 from the University of Southern California, 31 from Michigan, and 25 from Ohio State. Not surprising at all, right? Yet there also were 25 from Yale, 24 from Army, and 24 from Princeton. That speaks to the length and breadth of the college game over the century-plus of its existence. The College Football hall captures it all.

The hall originated in Kings Mill, Ohio, in 1978 and moved to South Bend, Indiana, in 1995, but since 2014 it has been situated in the heart of Atlanta's sports, tourism, and entertainment district. It holds three floors of excellence that include more than 50 interactive exhibits and one must-see three-story wall that features the helmets of nearly

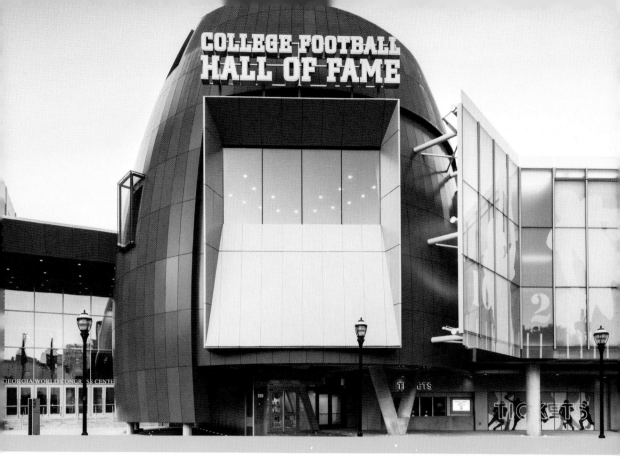

800 schools that play the game. The Chick-fil-A Peach Bowl Skill Zone allows visitors to attempt field goals, test their throwing accuracy, and run an obstacle course that, in most cases, leaves their once-able bodies in heaps. But this also is where iconic names are immortalized: Red Grange, Jim Thorpe, Archie Griffin, Dick Butkus, Herschel Walker, Bo Jackson . . . the list goes on and on. If you love college football—and especially if you count yourself among those who prefer it to the NFL—you have to see this place.

CANADIAN FOOTBALL LEAGUE HALL OF FAME

FROM 1972 UNTIL 2015, the Canadian hall was one of the more recognizable buildings in Hamilton, Ontario. A freestanding structure beside the former Hamilton City Hall, it featured a large metal sculpture called *Touchdown* out front and some 80,000 artifacts and busts of nearly 300 Canadian Football League players inside. A virtual exhibit highlighted, in the words of the hall, "the shared history of the game of football in North America, and how our distinctly Canadian style of play came to be relative to our neighbors to the south." Alas, attendance dwindled to such an extent that the hall eventually closed, forced to put its wares into storage.

Thus endeth the bad news. Starting in 2017, the hall will live at the north end of Tim Hortons Field, home of the eight-time Grey Cup–winning Hamilton Tiger-Cats. Take it in

if you can, and learn about not only the CFL greats—Doug Flutie, Warren Moon, and Bud Grant among them—but about the stars of Canadian university football and the national amateur Canadian Junior Football League. By the way, Flutie and Moon are on every list of the top quarterbacks in CFL history, but so are guys named Anthony Calvillo, Damon Allen, Ron Lancaster, and Tracy Ham. Why not get to know them?

» Hall of Fame running backs Tony Dorsett and Jim Brown were inducted into their teams' Rings of Honor. Bigger honor? That's not for us to say.

NFL RINGS OF HONOR

LIKE SO MANY of the proudest traditions associated with the Dallas Cowboys, the first NFL Ring of Honor, at the erstwhile Texas Stadium in Irving, was the brainchild of the franchise's original president and general manager, Tex Schramm. The Cowboys' Ring of Honor now circles an upper facade at AT&T Stadium in Arlington, with Schramm's name among those of 19 other America's Team legends.

By now, most NFL teams have some version of a Ring of Honor, many of them called just that and displayed in similar fashion, though there's much variation among them. The Washington Redskins' Ring of Fame at FedEx Field numbers a whopping 47 inductees, many more than the New Orleans Saints' four-strong Ring of Honor (though one suspects Drew Brees will soon make it a fivesome). The Kansas City Chiefs have added one name to the Arrowhead Stadium Ring of Honor every year (except for 1983) since 1970, while the Pride of the Jaguars in Jacksonville numbers only four. The New York

Jets and New York Giants both have Rings of Honor at MetLife Stadium, but removable placards are used so that the correct team's immortals are honored depending on which team is playing.

The Miami Dolphins have their Honor Roll, the Buffalo Bills their Wall of Fame, and the Baltimore Ravens a Ring of Honor that includes greats of the bygone Baltimore Colts. The Green Bay Packers have affixed the names of their six players with retired jerseys— most recently, Brett Favre—above the north end zone at Lambeau Field. All of the above, quite the sights to see.

LOST TO HISTORY

>> # IN HONOR OF MECCAS LOST TO HISTORY

THE HOUSTON ASTRODOME hasn't had an NFL team since 1996, yet there it remains—a giant, flying saucer–shaped question mark. The latest big idea was to convert it into a parking garage. The Pontiac Silverdome, home to the Detroit Lions until 2001, by late 2016 had sat unused for years, its roof decayed and its barren field a hideous wasteland.

Sometimes, the humane thing to do is blow a place to smithereens. That's what was done in 2008 to the RCA Dome in Indianapolis, home to the NFL Colts from 1984 to 2007, and in 2014 to the Metrodome in Minneapolis, home to the NFL Vikings from 1982 to 2013 and the University of Minnesota from 1982 to 2008. So, too, were these four iconic football stadiums demolished in recent years:

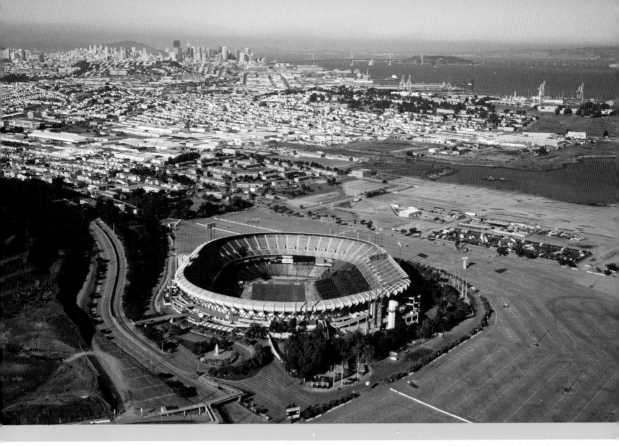

Miami Orange Bowl. Little Havana's home to many star-laden Miami Dolphins squads (until 1986) and some great University of Miami teams (until 2007)—not to mention one of college football's most prestigious bowl games—was demolished in 2008.

Texas Stadium. The Dallas Cowboys played in Irving from 1971 to 2008. Unique due to its fixed partial roof, which shaded the stands but allowed the field to shine in the sunlight, it was demolished in 2009.

Giants Stadium. With the New York Giants as tenants for 34 seasons and the New York Jets for 26, it hosted more NFL games than any other stadium. Demolition came in 2010.

Candlestick Park. The 49ers played on the wind-whipped western shores of the San Francisco Bay from 1971 to 2013. The stadium—originally built for baseball's Giants, but best known for the eight NFC Championship Games it hosted—was demolished in 2015.

CHAPTER 2

BAD BLOOD

THEY GO TOGETHER not like oil and water, but rather like leaking gas and an open flame. Football's best rivalries — Bears-Packers, Michigan-Ohio State, and all the others herein — explode with emotion and physical play on the field, and with opposing loyalties off it. Yet they also fit together like pieces of a beautiful puzzle, neither side truly whole without the other. The best part: It happens every year, in some cases more than once.

 NFL Rivalries
- ► Bears vs. Packers
- ► Cowboys vs. Redskins
- ► Broncos vs. Raiders
- ► Eagles vs. Giants
- ► Ravens vs. Steelers

College Football Rivalries

Dirty Dozen Major College Home-and-Homes
- ► The Game: Michigan vs. Ohio State
- ► Iron Bowl: Alabama vs. Auburn
- ► Jeweled Shillelagh: Notre Dame vs. USC
- ► Bedlam: Oklahoma vs. Oklahoma State
- ► Holy War: BYU vs. Utah
- ► Paul Bunyan's Axe: Minnesota vs. Wisconsin
- ► Palmetto Bowl: Clemson vs. South Carolina
- ► Big Game: Cal vs. Stanford
- ► Egg Bowl: Ole Miss vs. Mississippi State
- ► Civil War: Oregon vs. Oregon State
- ► Clean, Old-Fashioned Hate: Georgia vs. Georgia Tech
- ► Golden Boot: Arkansas vs. LSU

 Doing the Splits at Neutral-Sites with 50/50 Crowds
➤ Red River Rivalry: Oklahoma vs. Texas
➤ World's Largest Outdoor Cocktail Party: Florida vs. Georgia
➤ Army vs. Navy

The HBCUs: Historically Black Colleges and Universities
➤ Bayou Classic: Grambling State vs. Southern
➤ Florida Classic: Bethune-Cookman vs. Florida A&M
➤ Magic City Classic: Alabama State vs. Alabama A&M

Old School
➤ The (Other) Game: Harvard vs. Yale
➤ The Rivalry: Lafayette vs. Lehigh

High School Rivalries
➤ Mater Dei vs. Servite (California)
➤ Male vs. Manual (Kentucky)
➤ Don Bosco Prep vs. Bergen Catholic (New Jersey)
➤ Canton McKinley vs. Massillon Washington (Ohio)
➤ Jenks vs. Union (Oklahoma)

>> Bears-Packers rivalry greats Brian Urlacher and Brett Favre appear to share a warmish moment (what were they thinking?) after a game.

BEARS VS. PACKERS

IT'S THE NFL'S most-played rivalry, dating back to 1921, and what sustains it are the deep-seated differences between the fan bases. The City of Big Shoulders vs. small-town Dairyland. Giardiniera vs. sauerkraut. The volatile emotions of Bears fans vs. the unbreakable pro-Packers spirit.

A guaranteed two games a year in the NFC North doesn't hurt, nor does the history of affronts that flows both ways along the 208-mile path separating Lambeau Field and Soldier Field. The Bears owned the 1940s and '50s and later made a mockery of the Packers during Mike Ditka's time as coach. The Packers ruled the '60s and have enjoyed rampant rivalry success in the Brett Favre–Aaron Rodgers era.

Dick Butkus. Ray Nitschke. William Perry blasting across the goal line on *Monday Night Football*. Charles Martin injuring Jim McMahon with a body slam. All this history carries over into the games played today, where pilgrimages to one stadium or the other titillate visiting fans—who understand just how unwelcome they will be.

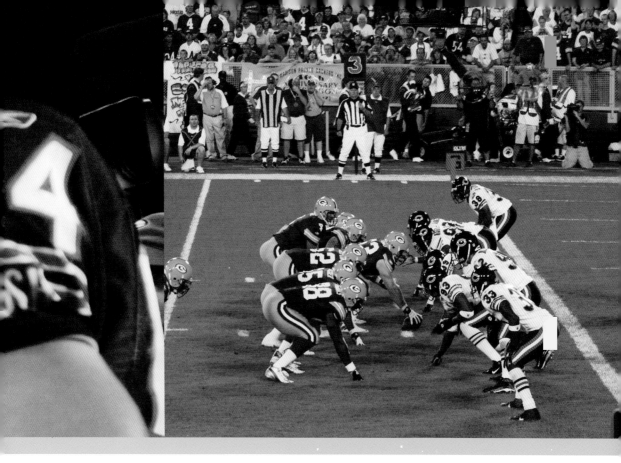

To attend a Bears-Packers game—or Packers-Bears, if you prefer—is indeed to dive headlong into the history of pro football in America. Such weightiness can make or break the reputation of a player (Jay Cutler, anyone?). Yet that sense of cultural import is what sets this rivalry apart from any other.

SHOUT OUT

"I remember playing the Packers in a preseason game [in 1984] up at County Stadium in Milwaukee. The way the field was configured, we had to share the same sideline with them—and you had two head coaches who really, and I mean really, didn't like each other. So you had Mike Ditka standing on his 49-yard line and Forrest Gregg standing on his 49-yard line, and they spent the whole game yelling expletives at each other. A couple times, we had to hold Ditka back. The rivalry got uglier for a while after that."

—Dan Hampton, Bears defensive lineman (1979–90)

≫ In the early 1970s, the Cowboys-Redskins rivalry heated up big-time—even an all-time great quarterback like Roger Staubach was going to get drilled.

COWBOYS VS. REDSKINS

THERE IS SOMETHING highly evocative—if politically incorrect—about this pairing, but what got this rivalry off the ground in the 1970s had little to do with contrived cowboys-and-Indians imagery. Rather, it was precious stuff like Redskins coach George Allen being accused of spying on Dallas practices, Cowboys Cliff Harris and Charlie Waters brawling with fans in the stands in Washington, and Cowboys star Harvey Martin flinging a funeral wreath into the Redskins locker room after a victory. Some mighty good football was played, too, with these distant NFC East partners combining to win eight Super Bowls from the 1971 through 1995 seasons.

To be sure, fans in Washington, DC—like those in New York and Philadelphia—have long delighted in portraying the Cowboys as geographical and cultural outliers. The audacity the Cowboys show in calling themselves "America's Team" never has played well in our nation's capital. But the beauty of 'Boys fans in Big D and beyond: They're bold and brash and utterly proud of it.

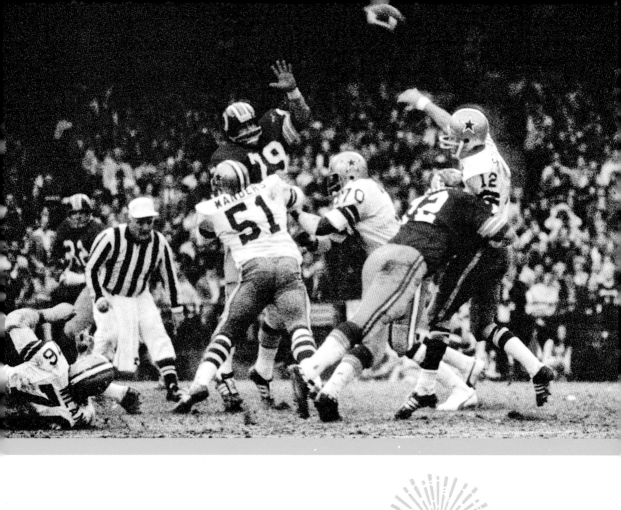

FedEx Field's girth and the Land-over, Maryland, location still make some fans long for the city-based charms of old RFK Stadium, where the 'Skins stopped playing in 1996. The Cowboys' billion-dollar stadium upgrade in 2009 was a major game-changer; as many as 105,000 now pile into AT&T Stadium in Arlington, Texas, on Sundays.

> The Broncos' John Elway was a central figure in his team's rivalry with the Raiders from the time the latter team tried— to no avail—to move up in the draft to select him.

BRONCOS VS. RAIDERS

THE TEAMS have been division rivals since their American Football League days, when the Raiders routinely hammered the Broncos to the tune of a 15–4–1 record in the 1960s, leading into the AFL-NFL merger. From 1970 forward, the Raiders piled on in AFC West matchups, winning 11 of the first 13. It all changed—a rivalry born—in 1977, when the Broncos were victorious in Oakland, ending the defending Super Bowl champs' 17-game winning streak. Denver doubled down by beating the Raiders in the AFC Championship Game en route to its first Super Bowl.

The real froth came in the 1980s, first when controversial Raiders owner Al Davis tried unsuccessfully to trade for a No. 1 overall draft pick so he could select Stanford's John Elway; Davis was convinced NFL commissioner Pete Rozelle secretly subverted the deal. Later came the Mike Shanahan kerfuffle: Davis fired his head coach during the '89 campaign, only to see him snapped up by the Broncos as an offensive assistant. Shanahan became Denver's head coach in 1995 and, along with Elway, won two Super Bowls.

What has unfurled through the years is a cultural head-butting between the opposing fan bases, seeming haves vs. have-nots. Stadium-wise, it's no contest: Denver's Mile High glory vs. Oakland's run-down baseball venue, a blight on the league. There's a general thumbing-of-the-nose from one side, resentment from the other. Tension, baby.

>> Just another Sunday steeped in rivalry stew for Giants quarterback Eli Manning, who has absorbed more than his share of hits from Eagles defenders through the years.

EAGLES VS. GIANTS

THE RIVALRY dates back to 1933; each team has won roughly the same number of times as the other. But the Super Bowl title scoreboard reads Giants 4, Eagles 0. That pushes bile from Philly's Lincoln Financial Field every inch of the 95-mile northeasterly path to MetLife Stadium. What comes in return is laughter, scorn, and dismissiveness.

Yet the Eagles have dominated the series in recent years; they won 13 of 16 games from the second meeting of 2008 through the end of the 2015 season. If Giants quarterback Eli Manning were judged on his performance versus Philadelphia, he'd be seen as the mother of all busts. Instead, he has won the mother of all games—the Super Bowl—twice.

Philadelphians have been said to suffer from an inferiority complex when it comes to their relationship with New Yorkers. A better way to describe it—at least where Eagles meet Giants—is that the good folks of Philly thrill in nothing else as they do in taking

down the Big Blue. Game days in this series never disappoint where emotions are concerned, and both venues are first-rate. It's easy to travel between the cities by rail or by bus, and the to-do list is long once you get to either destination. If a football game is the cornerstone of the trip, all the better.

"It's the people [of Philadelphia]. We don't have to deal with it as much, but when you come back, your families tell you all the stories about stuff that happened in the stands. It is, hands down, a gritty, grimy city and they love their team and they are willing to support and they do it in their own special way."

— Mathias Kiwanuka,
Giants defensive end (2006–14)

>> The physical nature of Ravens-Steelers is no joke. In a 2011 matchup (above), superstars Ray Lewis and Ben Roethlisberger embodied just how hard-hitting this rivalry is.

RAVENS VS. STEELERS

THE FOOTBALL UNIVERSE seems to be in steadfast agreement regarding the ferocity of this matchup: It is the angriest, hardest-hitting rivalry in the NFL. It's Steel City vs. Charm City—hold the charm. Nothing else quite measures up to the live-wire tension that's created when the bash brothers of the AFC North share the field.

From 2009 through 2013, nine of the teams' ten regular-season matchups were decided by three points or less—a rivalry run so unthinkably good that Ravens-Steelers shot to the top of many best-in-the-NFL lists. If there was a defining year, it may have been 2010. In Week 4 of that season, the Ravens traveled to Pittsburgh and handed the Steelers their first defeat, in a 17–14 slugfest. Nine weeks later, the Steelers won 13–10—Baltimore's only loss during a stretch of 24 home games. Round 3 went to the Steelers, who trailed 21–7 in the divisional playoffs at home before rallying for a 31–24 victory.

Another classic: the 2013 Thanksgiving game, won by the Ravens, 22–20. Two late, apparent touchdowns by the Steelers were negated by replay. The enduring image, though, is of Pittsburgh coach Mike Tomlin standing in the field of play and obstructing return man Jacoby Jones's path to the end zone. Anger and spice: It's nice.

SHOUT OUT

"With the bad blood between us, the dislikes between us, there's an understanding — and the understanding is, we don't like each other."

— Ike Taylor, Steelers cornerback (2003–14)

>> From Bo and Woody to Ezekiel Elliott, with a host of star figures in between, the Game has been a rivalry dialed up to 10 since the start of the 1970s.

THE GAME: MICHIGAN VS. OHIO STATE

BY THE TIME Bo Schembechler was hired by Michigan in 1968, Woody Hayes had 18 seasons and three Rose Bowl victories under his belt at Ohio State—not to mention a 12–6 record against the Wolverines. There was a healthy rivalry between the schools, but it was nothing like what it would become. The "Ten-Year War" would change everything.

From 1969 to '78, Schembechler's program lost only 16 times and Hayes's program 19 times. No other Big Ten school during that period sniffed the Rose Bowl. The stakes when the Wolverines and Buckeyes played were enormous; during one six-year stretch, there were four meetings in which both teams were ranked in the top five nationally. Fueled by the outsized personalities of Bo and Woody, the Game grew in stature by the year and the animosity between the fan bases deepened.

Michigan-Ohio State seemingly has entered a new heyday, with elite coaches Jim Harbaugh in Ann Arbor and Urban Meyer in Columbus, and what fan wouldn't sign up for a

decade of that? The path between the schools' monstrous football stadiums still is under 200 miles long. Wolverines fans still view Ohio State as less dignified, and Buckeyes fans still see Michigan as the team that can't hold its own without pillaging towns south of the state line for recruits. All the elements of a top-notch rivalry remain wonderfully intact.

>> Iron icons: Auburn's Ralph "Shug" Jordan and Alabama's Paul "Bear" Bryant stood on opposite sidelines in Birmingham for nearly two decades. Their teams—seen here in 2010 (right)—still go at it.

>> IRON BOWL: ALABAMA VS. AUBURN

FOOTBALL ALLEGIANCES have been divided in the state since the 1940s, when the Alabama-Auburn game became an annual, neutral-site affair contested at Legion Field in Birmingham. From 1958 to '82—the Paul "Bear" Bryant years in Tuscaloosa—it was a mostly one-way street, with the Crimson Tide winning 19 of 25 along with a bundle of national championships. Second place in the Southeastern Conference typically was as good as life got for the Tigers.

Yet Auburn turned things around during the 1980s, winning six of eight meetings in one stretch—the first victory coming in Bryant's final Iron Bowl, on a Bo Jackson fourth-down touchdown in the waning moments. The rivalry is played on campus now, and the Tigers have held their own; from 2002 to 2007 they won six times in a row, fomenting outrage in Roll Tide Nation that led to the masterstroke hiring of Nick Saban. Of course, even the great Nicktator has tasted his share of Iron Bowl defeat, most notably Auburn's

Cam Newton–led comeback in 2010 at Bryant-Denny and the "Kick Six" classic in 2013 at Jordan-Hare.

These games stop time throughout the state, and quite a streak began in 2009 of the winner going on to the national title game or the College Football Playoff. Don't even try to tell an Alabamian the Iron Bowl isn't the No. 1 rivalry in the sport.

≫ What'll be added to the shillelagh next—an emerald-studded shamrock for an Irish victory or a ruby-adorned Trojan head for a USC win? The Trojans fell 20–16 in a rainy 2010 game.

JEWELED SHILLELAGH: NOTRE DAME VS. USC

IT'S HOLLYWOOD vs. the Heartland, and what could be more diametrically opposed than that? Yet what binds these rivals is how alike they are: From iconic coaches to Heisman Trophy winners and national championships, these have been two of the most relevant football schools in America over time.

The Jeweled Shillelagh—a Gaelic war club adorned with precious stones in the colors of the Irish and Trojans—is on the line each year, either the third Saturday of October in South Bend or the Saturday after Thanksgiving in Los Angeles. It's a trophy with an odd name, and it's a rivalry that itself is an oddity because of the distance between the schools and the fact that they don't share a conference. Yet the fan bases always have remained highly engaged, and they've sure taken turns stewing in defeat:

TOP THREE GAMES

1978: Trojans 27, Irish 25. Joe Montana carried Notre Dame all the way back from a 24–6 deficit and into the lead with 46 seconds left to play, but USC drove 50 yards in four plays to set up Frank Jordan's game-winning field goal.

1989: Irish 28, Trojans 24. The teams brawled on the field before the game, and USC taunted its No. 1–ranked hosts throughout. Yet Notre Dame, despite five turnovers, came up huge with 14 fourth-quarter points.

2005: Trojans 34, Irish 31. With the No. 1 Trojans trailing, Matt Leinart converted a 61-yard fourth-down pass to Dwayne Jarrett before scoring with three seconds left thanks to the "Bush Push"—a shove from behind by running back Reggie Bush.

Notre Dame had a 15–3–1 run from 1940 to '61 (the series lapsed for four years during World War II) and a 12–0–1 tear from 1983 to '95; USC was 11–2 from 1970 to '82 and 11–3 from 1996 to 2009.

BEDLAM: OKLAHOMA VS. OKLAHOMA STATE

WE SHOULD START by acknowledging that the action hasn't always lived up to the unbeatable "Bedlam" name; such is going to be the case when one side—Oklahoma—has outperformed the other by better than a five-wins-to-one ratio over the course of more than 100 years. More often than not, this has been a mismatch, though Oklahoma State cranked up the heat in unforgettable fashion beginning in 1995. After enduring a miserable stretch of nearly three decades in which they went 1–26–1, the Cowboys won five of the next eight contests. They've been persistent threats to the Sooners ever since.

>> Blue-blood Oklahoma wins more than its share of tussles with Oklahoma State, but the upset-minded Cowboys always are dangerous. And on those occasions when they knock off the Sooners, it's sheer bedlam.

TOP THREE GAMES

1988: Sooners 31, Cowboys 28. It was OSU's first time on national TV, and junior running back Barry Sanders captivated his audience with 215 rushing yards—but OU rallied for its 12th straight win in the series.

2001: Cowboys 16, Sooners 13. OU was ranked No. 4 and in line for a chance to repeat as national champ when the 3–7 Pokes—27-point underdogs in Norman—pulled off the biggest upset in Bedlam history.

2010: Sooners 47, Cowboys 41. The Sooners—in the strange position of being underdogs against No. 9 OSU in Stillwater—held on in a game that had "Bedlam" written all over it. The teams combined for 40 fourth-quarter points.

And make no mistake about this: Beating blue-blood Oklahoma—and its much larger contingent of fans—means everything to the Pokes. There's a big brother–little brother dynamic in play here, and little bro nearly always manages to get some good licks in.

HOLY WAR: BYU VS. UTAH

THE RIVALRY'S NICKNAME is highly evocative—too much so for many—though religion is undeniably woven into the fabric of the rivalry's schools and fan bases. BYU is owned and operated by the Church of Jesus Christ of Latter-day Saints; Utah is a public institution. Though the Utes team and community include large numbers of LDS members, there certainly are fans who drink alcohol at tailgates and generally enjoy tweaking Cougar sensibilities. From both sides, the judgment can be ungracious.

BYU wideout Austin Collie inflamed things after a close 2007 victory, saying: "Obviously, when you're doing what's right on and off the field, I think the Lord steps in and plays a part in it. Magic happens."

>> Friendly neighbors? Um, no. The live-wire emotions when the Cougars and Utes clash are intoxicating and sometimes uncomfortable.

It's a hell of an on-the-field affair, we should add. The schools were conference rivals from 1922 until Utah joined the Pac-12 in 2011. From 1972 to '92, BYU won 19 of 21 meetings. The Utes won 16 of the next 23.

TOP THREE GAMES

1978: Utes 23, Cougars 22.
A year earlier, BYU had poured it on in a blowout win, prompting Utes coach Wayne Howard to declare a "crusade" for revenge. It came in comeback fashion in Salt Lake City.

1993: Utes 34, Cougars 31.
A 55-yard Chris Yergensen field goal won it, after which stunned BYU players ran back onto the field to keep the Utes and their fans from tearing down a goalpost.

2006: Cougars 33, Utes 31.
"Beck to Harline"—an indelible moment occurred as John Beck drove BYU down the field late and found Jonny Harline wide open and on his knees in the end zone on the final play, the capper on an 8–0 Mountain West campaign.

PAUL BUNYAN'S AXE: MINNESOTA VS. WISCONSIN

IN 1906—when President Theodore Roosevelt got involved in an effort to curb violent injuries, even deaths, in football—certain rivalry games went unplayed. One of them was Minnesota-Wisconsin, and 1906 remains the only blip in the longest-running annual series in the sport, dating back to 1890.

The schools played for the Slab of Bacon before, in 1948, Paul Bunyan's Axe took hold as the trophy to end all trophies in that part of the country. For the next 60-plus years, the winning side would grab the axe—from whichever sideline upon which it resided—and take a victory lap before "chopping down" the goalposts. That tradition was

>> What says mutual respect quite like taking axe to goalpost in the other team's backyard? The Badgers have had that pleasure many times in recent years.

TOP THREE GAMES

1952: Badgers 21, Gophers 21.
It was the first of two straight 21–21 ties between the teams, but it nailed down Wisconsin's first trip to the Rose Bowl— huge after Minnesota's domi- nance in the 1930s and '40s.

1993: Gophers 28, Badgers 21.
A Minnesota team that fin- ished 4–7 handed the Badgers their only defeat of the season, in Minneapolis, costing them a shot at a national title.

2005: Badgers 38, Gophers 34.
Both teams were ranked, but Minnesota owned the second half—until Justin Kucek's punt was blocked and recovered by Ben Strickland in the back of the end zone with 30 seconds on the clock.

threatened in 2013, after the Badgers' 10th straight winning effort, when Gophers play- ers surrounded one of the goalposts and ca- lamity nearly ensued. Bucky Badger. Goldy Gopher. It's totally heartland, it's cheesier than all get-out—it's beautiful.

PALMETTO BOWL: CLEMSON VS. SOUTH CAROLINA

IT'S THE LONGEST-RUNNING annual series in the South—every year since 1909—which makes it hugely special given the importance of college football in that neck of the American woods. And the fact that these intrastate rivals haven't belonged to the same league since 1970, their last year together in the Atlantic Coast Conference, only adds to the territorial allure.

Through the years, there have been fights between groups of fans, colossal pranks, and even the hideous sight of a Clemson fan strangling a chicken on the field. There is no love lost between the Palmetto State rivals, and never was that more apparent than

>> Who needs conference implications? State pride is more than good enough in Palmetto country.

TOP THREE GAMES

1977: Tigers 31, Gamecocks 27.
With 49 seconds remaining, Jerry Butler rose impossibly high to pull in a 20-yard touchdown pass from Steve Fuller, clinching Clemson's first bowl berth in 18 years.

1984: Gamecocks 22, Tigers 21.
A rally from 21–3 down concluded with an 86-yard drive for the winning score—only after USC got to re-kick a missed PAT due to a Clemson penalty. It was the Cocks' first 10-win season.

2006: Gamecocks 31, Tigers 28.
Clemson had touchdowns of 76 (Jacoby Ford catch), 80 (C. J. Spiller run), and 82 yards (Jock McKissic interception return) in the first half—and a 14-point second-half lead—but blew the game.

in 2004—when an all-out on-field fight between the teams was so egregious, it led to each school announcing that it wouldn't accept an invitation to a bowl game. Indeed, it was an ugly way for Lou Holtz to go out as coach of the Gamecocks.

BIG GAME: CAL VS. STANFORD

WHAT DO YOU GET when two really bright student bodies set their sights on each other? A history of hoaxes and practical jokes so clever and colorful, they stand the test of time. Like the Cal students who stole the Stanford Axe in 1899 and evaded capture by ferrying with it to Alameda while police checked passengers on the ferry back to Berkeley. Or the Stanford students who posed as photographers at a Cal pep rally during Big Game week in 1930, only to heave smoke bombs into the crowd and finally steal back the Axe. The hijinks continue to this day.

The campuses are not quite 50 miles apart. Stanford Stadium—completely rebuilt in 2006—is charmingly small (seats about 50,000) with all the modern amenities.

TOP THREE GAMES

1924: Indians 20, Bears 20. Stanford—until 1972, known as the Indians—trailed 20–6 with five minutes to go, but rallied for a tie that sent it to its first Rose Bowl in 23 years.

1982: Bears 25, Cardinal 20. John Elway drove Stanford down the field for what appeared to be the winning score, but—c'mon, you've seen "The Play" a million times— Cal, lateraling the ball five times, returned the ensuing kickoff for a touchdown as time expired.

Large-scale renovations at Cal's Memorial Stadium were completed in 2012, turning one of the Pac-12's worst venues into one of its best. The Big Game isn't always a close game, but it's a blast.

1990: Cardinal 27, Bears 25. Stanford, trailing 25–24, went for two and failed. Despite the handful of ticks left on the clock, Cal fans stormed the field; the Bears were penalized 15 yards. Stanford executed an onside kick and drilled a long field goal for a shocking "Payback" win.

EGG BOWL: OLE MISS VS. MISSISSIPPI STATE

OLE MISS SUPPORTERS rushed the field after a one-point victory at Mississippi State in 1926 and tried to—what else?—take down a goalpost. Some home fans weren't having it, and full-scale fighting broke out on the field, leaving several injured. The following year, the schools competed for the Golden Egg trophy for the first time.

From the mid-1940s through the 1980s, the Rebels owned MSU on the field. From the 1990s on, though, things have been essentially dead even. As both programs improved dramatically in recent years, negativity between the fan bases rose to such levels that some writers—and even Rebels coach Hugh Freeze—opined that things had gone too far.

>> It's no yolk: The loser of the annual Ole Miss–Mississippi State set-to never fails to leave the field with egg on its face.

TOP THREE GAMES

1983: Rebels 24, Bulldogs 23.
It's known as the "Immaculate Deflection"—an incredible gust of wind that blew MSU's 27-yard field goal attempt straight up in the air and short of the crossbar in the final seconds.

1997: Rebels 15, Bulldogs 14.
The teams fought at the 50-yard line prior to the game, then battled to a frenetic finish. Ole Miss quarterback Stewart Partridge drove the visitors 64 yards in the last two minutes for a touchdown and game-winning two-point conversion.

1999: Bulldogs 23, Rebels 20.
MSU trailed 20–6 in the fourth quarter before tying it up late. Deep in its own territory with 20 seconds to go, Ole Miss foolishly attempted a long pass; Eugene Clinton's interception return set up Scott Westerfield's 44-yard field goal for the win.

"Never has the Ole Miss and Mississippi State rivalry been more toxic," wrote Hugh Kellenberger of the Jackson *Clarion-Ledger* in July 2016. "It's become mean-spirited, short-sighted and to the detriment of the state as a whole."

Meanness? Toxicity? Where do we sign?

CIVIL WAR: OREGON VS. OREGON STATE

ONE CAN ONLY imagine what the view of Oregon football looks like from less than 50 miles away in Corvallis, home to Oregon State. The Ducks have state-of-the-art football facilities and endless uniform combos and a long-solidified national brand, all of it enabled at least in part by the school's relationship with billionaire Nike cofounder and superstar alumnus Phil Knight. The Beavers? Theirs is a far more modest and typical existence. In Eugene, there's really no excuse not to win big. In Corvallis, it's difficult not to feel some resentment.

There were many decades (read: pretty much the entire 20th century) when there was no such gap between the schools' football programs, but lately there has been no doubt

» North vs. South? No, this Civil War is more about Haves vs. Have-Nots. Nothing makes the Beavers' teeth gnash like a clash with the privileged Ducks.

TOP THREE GAMES

1994: Ducks 17, Beavers 13. Visiting Oregon drove 70 yards for the go-ahead touchdown in the fourth quarter, then held on defense to clinch its first Pac-10 title and Rose Bowl berth in 37 years.

2000: Beavers 23, Ducks 13. The first matchup in which both teams were ranked in the top 10 went swimmingly for OSU, which put itself into the Fiesta Bowl and kept Oregon out of the Rose Bowl.

2009: Ducks 37, Beavers 33. One of college football's games of the year—dubbed the "War of the Roses" because the winner would go to the Rose Bowl—featured nearly 900 yards of offense and a dizzying six lead changes.

who's the favorite and who's the underdog. Each campus is an hour and a half from the beach and a short drive from Portland, yet when it comes to football they are a world apart. Nothing means more to the Beavers and their fans than a Civil War victory.

CLEAN, OLD-FASHIONED HATE: GEORGIA VS. GEORGIA TECH

IF THERE WAS a singular boiling point in this rivalry, it came after Georgia Tech left the Southeastern Conference in 1964, the last time it would share a league with its neighbor 70 miles to the east. In a nutshell: Georgia Tech regretted the decision and wanted back in, but Georgia did everything in its power to keep a reconciliation from happening.

To this day, you'll be hard-pressed to find a Georgia fan who will deign to acknowledge the Yellow Jackets as the school's biggest football rival. It's fair to say that utter

» Georgia won't call Georgia Tech its biggest rival, but you can bet it stung big-time when the Yellow Jackets took bites out of the Sanford Stadium hedges in 2014.

TOP THREE GAMES

1971: Bulldogs 28, Yellow Jackets 24.
On Thanksgiving Day in Atlanta, Georgia got the ball at its 35-yard line with 1:29 to play, converted a critical fourth-and-10, and scored with 14 seconds on the clock to clinch a spot in the Gator Bowl.

1999: Yellow Jackets 51, Bulldogs 48 (OT).
Favored Georgia fumbled at the Tech 2-yard line with 15 seconds left in regulation, choking away an instant-classic game in which the teams combined for over 1,100 yards of offense.

dislike flows in one direction, and a mindful disregard in the other. When Georgia Tech left the SEC, it was one game over .500 in its series with the Dogs; after Georgia's victory in 2015, it was 25 games under .500. Regrets, Georgia Tech has had a few.

2008: Yellow Jackets 45, Bulldogs 42.
In a rivalry-stoking upset in Athens, Tech rushed for over 400 yards and overcame a 16-point halftime deficit with a 26–0 third-quarter explosion.

» If you want to hoist the Golden Boot, you might first have to grab victory from the jaws of defeat. Games in this series have often been perilously close.

GOLDEN BOOT: ARKANSAS VS. LSU

ARKANSAS-LSU IS A unique member of this group of rivalry games because of its "newness": Though the schools have a joined history of football that dates back to 1901, and though they reside in border states, the Golden Boot series began only in 1996, four years after Arkansas joined LSU in the Southeastern Conference.

The games since then—from 1996 to 2008, played the day after Thanksgiving—have often been remarkably entertaining; from 2001 to 2013, 10 of 13 were decided by a single score. The Razorbacks and Tigers are division rivals, adding to the spice, each trying to succeed in the brutally competitive SEC West and, in recent seasons, sharing the yeoman's task of standing in opposition to the dominant University of Alabama.

TOP THREE GAMES

2002: Razorbacks 21, Tigers 20.
In the "Miracle on Markham"—named for the main street that runs past War Memorial Stadium in Little Rock—the Hogs drove 81 yards in three plays in the final half-minute to win.

2006: Tigers 31, Razorbacks 26.
Arkansas was ranked No. 5, with serious national title hopes, and star running back Darren McFadden rushed for 182 yards. But LSU zapped the Hogs' dreams in Little Rock.

2007: Razorbacks 50, Tigers 48 (3OT).
This time, LSU was No. 1 in the land. And this time, McFadden rushed for 206 yards and three touchdowns and threw for a fourth score. Epic payback.

If the rivalry needed a boost, it came in 2007 when then-LSU coach Les Miles mispronounced "Arkansas" as "Ar-KANSAS." On purpose, it's safe to assume. Such slights almost always are.

>> The 50-yard-lines separate burnt orange from crimson in the stands of the Cotton Bowl in Dallas. Big Tex, the 55-foot-tall figure that watches over the state fair, surely approves.

RED RIVER RIVALRY: OKLAHOMA VS. TEXAS

THIS GAME was once known as the Red River Shootout, an evocative moniker, to be sure, playing into the Wild West allure of this part of the country. Both sides decided in 2005, before the 100th playing of the rivalry, to drop "Shootout"—an admirable decision, given gun violence in America—but no name change was going to alter the heated nature of Sooners vs. Longhorns.

When these teams meet on the second Saturday of the Texas State Fair in October, it's just plain perfect. One team or the other, and often both, tends to be terrific. There are mighty conference implications in the Big 12. There's also great charm in the game's adherence to tradition; it would be easy to move it to the state-of-the-art Dallas Cowboys stadium in Arlington, but why mess with how special it is at the Cotton Bowl in Dallas? The backdrop of the fair makes this a spectacle like no other.

WHILE YOU'RE THERE

☑ **Pick a side. Because you have to. That means donning the colors—it's worth it.**

☑ **Indulge in the Texas State Fair grub. That means fried Coke. And fried Jell-O. Yes, fried Jell-O. It means fried everything. You can work it off when you get home.**

It's also a stunning visual display—half the stadium donned in Texas' burnt orange, the other in Oklahoma's crimson. And the series has been similarly even: From 1952 to 2016, in fact, it was dead even, with a few ties thrown in for good measure. There have been spectacular Saturdays along the way—10 top-five matchups from 1963 to 2008 come to mind—but the rankings and records almost don't even matter.

☑ **Appreciate Cotton Bowl Stadium, an old-fashioned relic. Even the Cotton Bowl—the bowl game—has ditched this joint for Jerry Jones's glorious building in Arlington. Cotton Bowl Stadium has sneaky charm, though, and this is important.**

WORLD'S LARGEST OUTDOOR COCKTAIL PARTY: FLORIDA VS. GEORGIA

THE UNOFFICIAL NAME of this series is said to have been coined by a newspaperman in the 1950s who watched fairly in dismay—mixed with two fingers of awe—as an intoxicated fan offered an alcoholic beverage to a police officer. Neither school uses the "Cocktail" moniker in any official way connected with the annual Southeastern Conference East division battle, preferring not to promote overindulgent drinking at Jacksonville Landing—the party-central plaza facing the St. Johns River—or at tailgates outside EverBank Field, home of the NFL Jaguars. Alas, the party rages on.

The stands are half Florida's blue and half Georgia's red, and the action on the field is soaked with tradition and gamesmanship. Like in 1995—on Georgia's home field, as the stadium in Jacksonville was undergoing renovations—when the Steve Spurrier–coached Gators

» PSA: Don't drink and ride (mechanical gators, that is).
Or do. Either way, the Florida-Georgia tussle on the field is
going to be serious business.

WHILE YOU'RE THERE

☑ Tailgate like you mean
it, and don't be in too big
of a hurry to enter the
stadium. There'll be over
80,000 in the seats and
at least that many more
outside who don't even
have tickets to the game.

☑ Check out the Touchdown
Showdown fan-fest on
the south side of the
stadium. Entrance is free,
and food and drink are
plentiful.

ran up the score and Spurrier said afterward that he'd
wanted to hang "half a hundred" on the Bulldogs.
Or in 2007, when Georgia's entire team rushed the
end zone to celebrate an early touchdown under or-
ders from then-coach Mark Richt. From 1971 to 1989
the Dogs ruled the rivalry, winning 15 of 19 games.
But Spurrier changed everything upon his arrival in
1990—declaring his intention to make Georgia fans
miserable, and he delivered, going 11–1. Since then,
things have shifted back to essentially even.

» Cadets and midshipmen march onto the field before piling into packed stands and going wild for their respective academy brethren—there's simply no other scene like it in sports.

ARMY VS. NAVY

FIRST, LET'S TALK about where you're going to take in this extraordinary event. And the answer is: We don't know. The rivalry has been played every year since 1899. Starting in 1932, all but 13 Army-Navy games have been in Philadelphia—where Lincoln Financial Field sits 147 miles by car from the United States Military Academy in West Point, New York, and 123 miles from the United States Naval Academy in Annapolis, Maryland. Now Army-Navy remains on the move to multiple venues across the United States.

But understand this: Location won't change a thing about college football's most unique and special rivalry game, which of late has taken place on the second Saturday of December—a week after the major conference championship games, with a stage all its own. The stands are split between cadets and midshipmen, and pride and respect hang heavy in the air and on the field. The Cadets and Middies never fail to give their all until

the final whistle, and when it's over the teams stand at attention while each alma mater is played.

Navy won every year from 2002 to 2015, only adding to the drama—one side raising the bar for service academy football, with the other becoming something of a valiant underdog. Army's streak-busting 2016 victory was just what this rivalry needed.

SHOUT OUT

"Navy wants to beat Army—there's no question about it—but the mutual respect on the field is the thing about this game that never changes. These are young people on both sides who have so much in common. No matter who wins or who loses, that never changes. It's what makes this rivalry so wonderful."

—Roger Staubach,
Navy quarterback (1962–64)

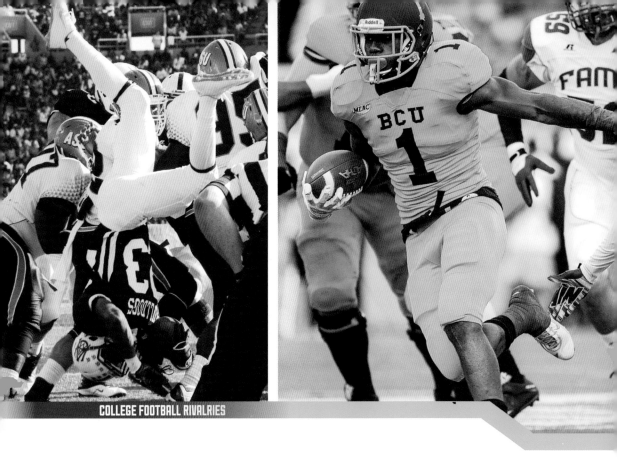

THE HBCUS

ALCORN STATE. Bethune-Cookman. Florida A&M. Grambling State. Hampton. Prairie View A&M. Southern. The names of America's Historically Black Colleges and Universities—these seven, and a hundred more—are familiar to most college football fans. On those occasions when an HBCU team lines up against a Football Bowl Subdivision opponent, it's probably an unfair fight. Yet when the HBCUs crash into one another, it's often a cultural splendor. Melee meets milieu, and everybody wins.

But enough about the bands. Seriously, the best college bands in the country don't reside at the giant football factories. Take in an HBCU rivalry game—maybe the **Bayou Classic** (Grambling State vs. Southern in New Orleans), the **Florida Classic** (Bethune-Cookman vs. Florida A&M in Orlando), or the **Magic City Classic** (Alabama A&M-Alabama State in Birmingham)—and you'll get your funk on while witnessing passionate football on the field.

The lifeblood of HBCU football can be found in the Mid-Eastern Athletic and Southwestern Athletic conferences. The MEAC is home to schools from Florida, Georgia, and

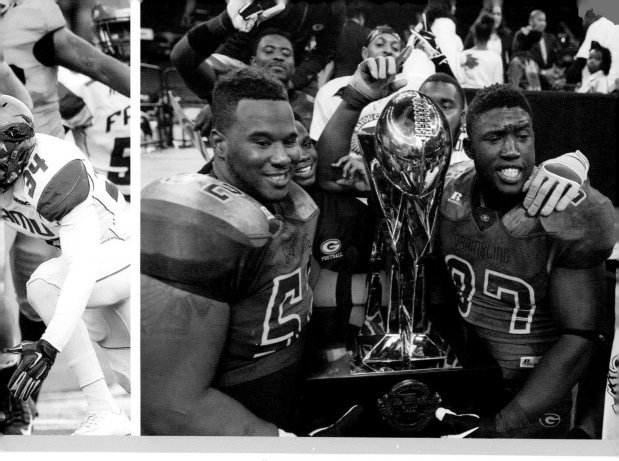

>> Scenes from recent Magic City Classic (Alabama A&M vs. Alabama State),
Florida Classic (Bethune-Cookman vs. Florida A&M), and Bayou Classic
(Grambling State vs. Southern) games—rivalry staples of the HBCU experience.

the Carolinas, and a bit of an outlier in Delaware State University. The SWAC footprint covers Alabama, Arkansas, Louisiana, Mississippi, and Texas. These are football states, and the rivalries therein are longstanding and rich in tradition. And then there are those bands—have we mentioned them?—which put all others to shame. HBCU football is something every football fan should experience.

THE BANDS

The monikers of the HBCU bands are musical and glorious. A 2016 poll done by the site HBCUBuzz.com, which attracted several thousand votes, ranked the University of Arkansas–Pine Bluff's Marching Musical Machine of the Mid-South at the top, followed by Prairie View A&M's Marching Storm, Jackson State's Sonic Boom of the South, and Southern's Human Jukebox. If those names don't make you want to revel in the stands, ask yourself what you've done wrong.

THE (OTHER) GAME*: HARVARD VS. YALE

OLD SCHOOL

* Or, the Game, depending on your point of view.

THIS RIVALRY IS SO OLD. (How old is it?) It's so old, the first meeting ended in a score of 4–0. It was in 1875, a pulse-quickening affair won by the Crimson. Back then, touchdowns weren't worth any points; it was the kick after pay dirt that was worth a single tally. The Game, as it's called—deal with it, Michigan and Ohio State—has come a long way since then.

Go to Harvard Stadium or the Yale Bowl on the last Saturday of the season nowadays, and you'll find fans of the Crimson and the Bulldogs tailgating together. It's fun and it's friendly enough—any we're-smarter-than-you tension in the air notwithstanding—but such is the charm of Ivy League football, where cutthroat intentions tend to be reserved for Monday through Friday. The Game itself has true extracurricular meaning for

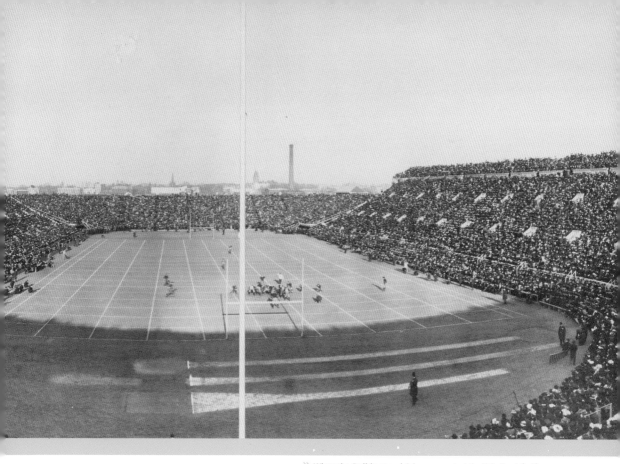

When the Bulldogs and Crimson meet at the Yale Bowl (left) or at Harvard Stadium (right) it's a tribute to history. The rivalry began in 1875, thirty years before the matchup shown at right.

the teams and alumni, which makes it special. You won't necessarily find raucous student sections at either stadium—tons of students keep the party going outside throughout the game—but that hardly matters. History drips inside the stadium walls.

Harvard is experiencing a boom time in the rivalry, having won 14 of 15 games from 2001 to 2016. ESPN got involved in 2014, sending its *College GameDay* production to Boston for the Crimson's 31–24 victory. Go for the fan signage, which itself is brilliant and often hilarious; in 2004, for example, a group of Yale students dressed as Harvard fans and convinced thousands of unwitting Crimson supporters to hold up red or white placards that, all together, spelled out "We suck." Or one from that 2014 game: "My first sign was too erudite for you uncouth ruffians."

THE RIVALRY: LAFAYETTE VS. LEHIGH

OLD SCHOOL

LET'S BEGIN WITH the superlative that authenticates Lafayette-Lehigh in every conceivable way: It is the most-played rivalry in all of college football. The Pennsylvania schools met on the field 152 times from 1884 through the 2016 contest, with 1896 being the only year they didn't play each other (but you knew that already). Only 17 miles separate Lafayette College in Easton from Lehigh University in Bethlehem, and naturally they share a conference—the Patriot League, since 1986. Each program has claimed a significant share of league titles, often with their battle deciding things.

There have been several classics during the Patriot years, none more dramatic than the 1995 game, when Lehigh stormed back from a 16-point fourth-quarter deficit at home to win in double overtime with the league title on the line. On the other hand, Lafayette in

>> It's a hop, skip, and a jump from Easton to Bethlehem—so close, in fact, it's no wonder these schools' football teams don't have much use for each other.

2005 hit on a 37-yard touchdown pass with 38 seconds remaining to win the Patriot; that was pretty good, too. Lafayette leads the overall series, but the back-and-forth along the way has been close enough to .500 to keep bragging rights partial.

This is Football Championship Subdivision football at its most celebrated; the Rivalry always is a sellout. Lafayette's Fisher Field has been home to the Leopards since 1926. A full-scale renovation completed in 2007 made this a real diamond in the rough—a wonderful place to take in a game. The Mountain Hawks' Goodman Stadium has the scenic backdrop of South Mountain. Each school touts its football environment as the very best the Patriot has to offer. Biased much? Both are terrific.

>> McKinley won this battle, but Massillon won the war. No, not the entire War of 1894—just the 2016 game, by a final score of 21–19.

>> HIGH SCHOOL RIVALRIES

THERE ARE SO MANY high school football rivalries across America that are steeped in tradition and fueled by passion. Here are five of the finest:

California: Mater Dei vs. Servite. Tremendous football is played throughout Orange County's Trinity League, yet Monarchs vs. Friars is the game—typically played at Angel Stadium in Anaheim—that looms above all others. When the MLB Angels make the play-offs, either Mater Dei hosts at the Santa Ana Bowl or Servite hosts at Cerritos College's Falcon Field. Both schools have produced many pros, and Mater Dei's list includes a pair of Heisman–winning quarterbacks: Notre Dame's John Huarte and USC's Matt Leinart.

Kentucky: Male vs. Manual. The Louisville public high schools sit just 5 miles apart via Interstate 65 and have been playing each other in football since 1893. For nearly a century, the Old Rivalry—some prefer to call it the Battle for the Barrel—occurred on Thanksgiving Day, but now it's in October. The Male Bulldogs and Manual Crimsons (note the plural spelling) have played at neutral sites to accommodate large crowds, but their on-campus set-tos are even better.

>> Union players hoist the state championship trophy
after beating Jenks in 2009.

New Jersey: Don Bosco Prep vs. Bergen Catholic. Each school is in the mid-teens in state championships. They are 10 miles apart, close enough to whip everybody involved into a frenzy. The Don Bosco Ironmen have it all in terms of resources. So do the Bergen Crusaders. Watch your elbows—they're likely to bump into a major-college recruiter.

Ohio: Canton McKinley vs. Massillon Washington. The rivalry is known as the War of 1894, which should give you a pretty good idea of how long it has been around. They play for the Victory Bell and each school boasts many notable football alumni. Coaches Wayne Fontes, Josh McDaniels, and Don Nehlen all hail from McKinley, which plays its games at Fawcett Stadium, adjacent to the Pro Football Hall of Fame. Massillon spawned coaches Paul Brown, Earle Bruce, and Don James and linebacker Chris Spielman.

Oklahoma: Jenks vs. Union. It's the Backyard Brawl, city (Union) vs. suburb (Jenks). Union's stadium is state of the art—and Jenks' is pretty darn nice—yet most of these games are contested on the University of Tulsa's field. State title implications are commonplace on both sides.

CHAPTER 3

NO PLACE LIKE HOME

BUILD IT, and they will come. This is true of the grandest stadiums in college football, eight of which hold more than 100,000 fans. It's true of stadiums, new and old, at every level of the sport that are truly unique, as you'll discover in this chapter. No two venues in football are exactly alike, and if fields of blue and red—and a pirate ship—don't demonstrate that, what could? Behold and enjoy.

The Eight Hundred Club: Over 100,000 Capacity. Only in College Football.
- ➤ The Big House (Michigan)
- ➤ Beaver Stadium (Penn State)
- ➤ Ohio Stadium (Ohio State)
- ➤ Kyle Field (Texas A&M)
- ➤ Neyland Stadium (Tennessee)
- ➤ Tiger Stadium (LSU)
- ➤ Bryant-Denny Stadium (Alabama)
- ➤ Darrell K. Royal Memorial Stadium (Texas)

One-of-a-Kind
- ➤ U.S. Bank Stadium (Minneapolis)
- ➤ Michie Stadium (Army at West Point)
- ➤ McLane Stadium (Baylor)
- ➤ Fargodome (North Dakota State)
- ➤ Eagle Stadium (Allen, Texas)
- ➤ Monument Valley Stadium (Monument Valley, Utah)
- ➤ Stadium Bowl (Tacoma, Washington)

Sightseeing
- ➤ The Scoreboard at AT&T Stadium in Arlington, Texas
- ➤ The Pirate Ship in Tampa
- ➤ The Blue Turf at Albertsons Stadium in Boise, Idaho
- ➤ The Red Turf at Roos Field Eastern Washington
- ➤ Walter Camp Gate at Yale Bowl

THE BIG HOUSE: MICHIGAN STADIUM [ANN ARBOR]

FIELDING YOST, the all-time-great coach whose Michigan teams won six national championships from 1901 through 1923, was an innovator as an administrator. The school's athletic director after he hung up his whistle, Yost envisioned a football stadium that could host many more fans than the 40,000 or so the

STADIUM CAPACITY

107,601

Wolverines played before at Ferry Field; he dared to think in six-figure terms. That was more than university regents would go in for, but when Michigan Stadium opened at Main Street and Stadium Boulevard in Ann Arbor in 1927, it seated 84,401—making it the largest college-owned stadium in the nation. It wasn't until 1955 that the stadium topped the 100,000 mark, and not until the 1980s that it became popularly known as the Big House.

The Big House is the largest stadium in the U.S. and second only to the national stadium in Pyongyang, North Korea, worldwide. Most of the stadium sits below ground level,

≫ The Big House is—what's that word again?—big.
Make that incredibly big. So big, no football fan
should miss a chance to see it.

which means the full view sneaks up on you as you approach on foot; it is a breathtaking sight. There are noisier venues; the roars seem to rise up and out of the building rather than hammer down onto the field. Of course, Michigan's critics maintain that it's because the school's fans are too bookish and snobby to get properly rowdy. Jealous much?

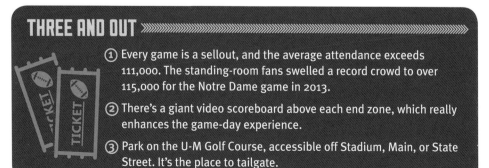

THREE AND OUT ≫≫≫≫≫≫≫≫≫≫≫≫≫≫≫≫≫≫≫≫≫≫≫≫≫≫≫

① Every game is a sellout, and the average attendance exceeds 111,000. The standing-room fans swelled a record crowd to over 115,000 for the Notre Dame game in 2013.

② There's a giant video scoreboard above each end zone, which really enhances the game-day experience.

③ Park on the U-M Golf Course, accessible off Stadium, Main, or State Street. It's the place to tailgate.

BEAVER STADIUM
(UNIVERSITY PARK, PENNSYLVANIA)

PENN STATE University's iconic football stadium came from humble origins. In 1960, 30,000-seat New Beaver Field was dismantled and moved from the west side of campus to the east end and put back together there to accommodate roughly 46,000 fans; the reconfigured version still stands as the lower bowl of the current facility. The football program's success over ensuing decades led to several rounds of stadium projects that brought capacity into the 90,000s. Prior to the 2001 campaign, another expansion pushed capacity over 100,000 with new scoreboards, additional restrooms and concession areas, and many other improvements. The end product: easily one of the best college venues anywhere.

STADIUM CAPACITY

106,572

As the Penn State community has put some distance between it and a giant scandal involving former longtime assistant coach Jerry Sandusky and the school that employed—

some would add "enabled"—him, the joy of football Saturdays has been renewed. The massive student section here, between the 10-yard lines in the south end of the stadium, is easily one of the best in the land. When Zombie Nation's techno mega-hit "Kernkraft 400" blasts through the loudspeakers after big plays by the Nittany Lions, the fans dance like delightful fools.

THREE AND OUT

1. Standing-room crowds have carried attendance over 110,000 on many occasions, giving Michigan Stadium a run for its money.

2. Go for a "whiteout" game if you can. There is one each season, and the visual of 100,000-plus clad in blinding white is powerful.

3. Getting to State College—far from everywhere—is no picnic. Plan your travel extra early.

OHIO STADIUM (COLUMBUS)

THE FANS IN the south end yell, "O!" The east, "H!" The north, "I!" And the west, "O!" It spells timeless tradition, gridiron excellence, and we're-just-plain-better-than-you-and-you-know-it. On the banks of the Olentangy River, Ohio Stadium is home to the big, bad Buckeyes of Ohio State University, a football giant that looms as large as any on the college landscape—and the stadium itself more than measures up. A nearly $200 million refurbishment completed in 2001 made the on-campus "Shoe" a top-of-the-line place to see a game, though it probably was that already; since 1949, OSU never has ranked lower than fourth nationally in average home attendance.

STADIUM CAPACITY

104,944

Fans here are—how to put this delicately?—insane for the Buckeyes. They pile into every seat, nook, and cranny of the double-deck horseshoe-designed stadium, which provides a closeness to the field that's hugely intimidating to opponents and views that are splendid no matter where one sits. "Horseshoe" suggests an open end, but that's not

> Technically, the "horseshoe" exists no more in Columbus—
not that Buckeyes fans are complaining about this massive,
intimidating structure. O! H! I! Whoa!

the case here; what used to be temporary bleachers in the south end now is fixed seating, with openings at the edges that preserve the horseshoe feel. When "Seven Nation Army" by the White Stripes pipes in before kickoffs and after big plays by the Buckeyes, forget about it—it's bonkers. You won't find more dedicated, engaged football fans anywhere.

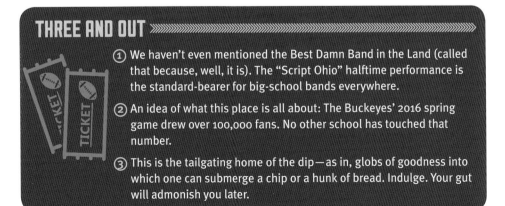

THREE AND OUT »»»»»»»»»»»»»»»»»»»»»»»»»»»»»»»»»»»»»

① We haven't even mentioned the Best Damn Band in the Land (called that because, well, it is). The "Script Ohio" halftime performance is the standard-bearer for big-school bands everywhere.

② An idea of what this place is all about: The Buckeyes' 2016 spring game drew over 100,000 fans. No other school has touched that number.

③ This is the tailgating home of the dip—as in, globs of goodness into which one can submerge a chip or a hunk of bread. Indulge. Your gut will admonish you later.

KYLE FIELD
(COLLEGE STATION, TEXAS)

HULLABALOO, *Caneck! Caneck!* If those words don't mean anything to you, consider yourself in league with most of the fans at Texas A&M University. The close of the "Aggie War Hymn"—*Chig-gar-roo-garem, Chig-gar-roo-garem, Rough Stuff! Texas A&M!*—doesn't make a whole lot of plain sense, either, yet it hardly matters, because this is the mother of all fight songs. After the second verse is sung, Aggies fans link their arms and legs and sway, causing the upper deck to move so dramatically that first-timers seated there can do little more than pray to the gods of architecture.

STADIUM CAPACITY

102,733

After joining the gold-standard Southeastern Conference in 2012, Texas A&M committed to full-scale renovations at Kyle Field. Both sides of the stadium were demolished and rebuilt in time for the 2015 opener. The process increased capacity by approximately

>> The higher up you sit at Kyle Field, the more you'll be shaken during the "Aggie War Hymn." Try not to be stirred.

20,000, making Kyle Field No. 1 in the SEC in this category. It also introduced a new upper level on the south end of the stadium and substantial improvements to the exterior grounds. Total cost for all this: an estimated $450 million.

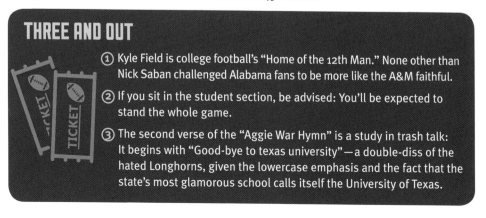

THREE AND OUT

① Kyle Field is college football's "Home of the 12th Man." None other than Nick Saban challenged Alabama fans to be more like the A&M faithful.

② If you sit in the student section, be advised: You'll be expected to stand the whole game.

③ The second verse of the "Aggie War Hymn" is a study in trash talk: It begins with "Good-bye to texas university"—a double-diss of the hated Longhorns, given the lowercase emphasis and the fact that the state's most glamorous school calls itself the University of Texas.

THE EIGHT HUNDRED CLUB

NEYLAND STADIUM
(KNOXVILLE, TENNESSEE)

BY THE HUNDREDTH time you hear the Pride of the Southland Band play "Rocky Top," the song made famous by the University of Tennessee Volunteers, you'll have joined in the singing long ago. What you need to know here are the words to a simple chorus:

> *Rocky top, you'll always be*
> *Home sweet home to me.*
> *Good ole rocky top,*
> *Rocky top Tennessee, rocky top Tennessee.*

It's an ode to the Great Smoky Mountains. Listen for the howls of Smokey the Bluetick Coonhound, the live mascot that embodies so much of the aforementioned tradition. Drink in the majesty of the orange-and-white checkerboard end zones, which simply are

STADIUM CAPACITY

102,455

>> Whether or not the Vols are in contention in the Southeastern Conference,
the house will be full, "Rocky Top" will be sung (and sung), and—
somewhere amid all that orange—Smokey will be howling.

the coolest in all of college football. Thrill as the Vols race onto the field through the T

formed by the marching band in a stadium the *Sporting News* ranked No. 1 in college

football *before* the $100 million-plus in renovations completed in 2010. Will folks here be

waiting forever for the next Peyton Manning? Sure. It only adds to their charm.

THREE AND OUT

① Don't you dare miss the Vol Walk—when the team heads from the
Torchbearer statue in Circle Park and up Peyton Manning Pass, all
the way to the stadium. The band and cheerleaders will be there.

② Tailgating is mighty fine here. Think ribs. It's the SEC, is it not?

③ You're less than an hour from Great Smoky Mountains National Park.
Make time for this must-do excursion.

>> Tiger Stadium has grown in volume—from a capacity of 12,000 to more than eight times that number—and in volume. It gets no louder in college football.

>> TIGER STADIUM
(BATON ROUGE, LOUISIANA)

LEGENDARY ALABAMA coach Bear Bryant called this the "worst place in the world" for a visiting team to have to play. The experience was like being "inside a drum." Yes, it's loud in Death Valley, as the on-campus stadium of Louisiana State University is known. It's so loud that game-winning moments have

STADIUM CAPACITY

102,321

been known to register at seismographic earthquake levels. Yes, this is the loudest stadium in college football. No, it's not officially such; it's not a matter of utmost certitude. But does anyone dare argue with it? If you've been to a game in Death Valley, you just *know*.

Opened in 1924 with a capacity of only 12,000, Tiger Stadium has grown . . . and grown. There have been seemingly endless projects to enlarge the stadium's capacity; only in 2014 did it leap above 100,000. But one needn't be bogged down by those details. It's about the volume, a byproduct of the incredible passion Tigers fans bring to the stadium game in and

game out. You'll never *feel* more than you do here. LSU's home games against its division foes in the Southeastern Conference—Alabama, Auburn, Arkansas, et al.—are spectacular theater. And there's always an ominous thickness in the air, perhaps due in part to the "Welcome to Death Valley" inscribed on the video board on the north end zone.

THREE AND OUT

1. It's a little thing that leaves a big impression: the numbers on the "5s" and not just the usual "10s." As in: "He's at the 30, the 25, the 20, the 15"—and so on.

2. Stop by the 15,000-square-foot enclosure where mascot Mike the Tiger lives. He may or may not answer to "Mike."

3. The Jack & Priscilla Andonie Museum, on University Lake a mile and a half from the stadium, celebrates all things LSU football. It's open on football Saturdays from 9 a.m. until three hours before kickoff.

BRYANT-DENNY STADIUM
(TUSCALOOSA, ALABAMA)

TWO WORDS: Roll Tide. Seriously, take those two words with you to Tuscaloosa—they're all you'll need. "Roll Tide" can be used to say hello, goodbye, and most things in between (think: "I do") in the football-obsessed hometown of the University of Alabama. Many of the best traditions involve music: the Crimson Tide running onto the field to AC/DC's "Thunderstruck"; the crowd singing along to "Dixieland Delight" by the group Alabama; of course, the fans waving their crimson-and-white pompons (they're called "shakers" here) while belting out "Roll, Tide, Roll!" in between lines of the chorus of Lynyrd Skynyrd's "Sweet Home Alabama." There's the school's Million Dollar Band. There's "Rammer Jammer." So many lyrics!

Bryant-Denny has undergone eight separate expansions since it opened in 1929, more than octupling its original capacity of 12,000. In time for the 2006 season, the north

STADIUM CAPACITY

101,821

Alabama's stadium certainly befits the premier program in college football. Attend a game here and be delighted—maybe even thunderstruck.

end zone area was modified, bringing capacity over 90,000, and display screens were added throughout the stadium. In time for the 2010 season, the south end was brought up to speed—and capacity to over 100,000.

THREE AND OUT

1. In 1975, the stadium was renamed—by the Alabama state legislature—to honor Paul "Bear" Bryant, who was still coaching the team at the time and would be for several more years.

2. The team enters the stadium two hours prior to kickoff via the Walk of Champions, a brick path connecting Bryant-Denny to University Boulevard.

3. Be sure to check out Denny Chimes, the 115-foot tower on the Quad at the center of campus. The handprints and footprints of every Tide football captain since 1948 are pressed into cement slabs at the base.

DARRELL K. ROYAL MEMORIAL STADIUM (AUSTIN, TEXAS)

AFTER ITS 13–1 campaign of 2009, which culminated in an appearance in the national championship game, the fortunes of the University of Texas football program plummeted. The Long-horns lost 21 games over Mack Brown's final four years as coach, and from 2014 to 2016 they had—unthinkably—back-to-back-to-back losing seasons under Brown's successor, Charlie Strong. By that point, sellouts at the Big 12 Conference's largest stadium no longer were the norm. Yet the next heyday never can be too far away at a school with all the inherent advantages.

Named for Hall of Fame coach Darrell Royal, who served in the army during World War II and later led Texas to three national titles, the stadium opened in 1924 (capacity: 27,000) and was dedicated to all Texans who had fought in the first World War. Expansion became routine over the years; when 4,000-plus permanent bleacher seats were added

STADIUM CAPACITY

100,119

>> Everything's bigger in Texas, right? That includes the angst among fans when the Longhorns aren't great, but no worries—game days in this stadium are giant events regardless. (Also: Austin is way cool.)

for the 2009 season, it bumped capacity over the magical 100,000 mark. All things here are Texas-big. Try to find a bigger, more imposing mascot than Bevo the longhorn steer, or a more astonishing bass drum than Big Bertha, the "star" of the Longhorn Band. Or a better song to sing with 100,000 friends than "The Eyes of Texas."

THREE AND OUT

① Say hello to "Godzillatron," the 7,370-square-foot LED scoreboard that was erected in 2006 and billed as the largest HD video screen in the world. For several years after it was surpassed (by a screen in Tokyo), it remained the largest HD screen in the western hemisphere.

② You have to know how to "Hook 'em"—extend your pointer and pinky fingers, and ball the rest of your hand into a fist.

③ There were recent plans to increase capacity to an unheard-of range between 115,000 and 125,000, but they were scuttled—temporarily.

» The glass paneling of the Vikings' new stadium is such a dramatic, dazzling departure from the drab Metrodome, it has beautified the Downtown East section of Minneapolis.

» U.S. BANK STADIUM
[MINNEAPOLIS]

WHO DOESN'T want to sit outside in Minnesota in the throes of early winter and watch football? Actually, the NFL Vikings wished for an outdoor stadium as they proposed plans for a building to replace the Metrodome, but state and local governments would provide funding only for another (albeit much-improved) indoor joint. And what a swanky joint this is, located in the Downtown East section of the city at the former site of the Dome. U.S. Bank Stadium (price tag: over $1 billion) is far too special not to be in the rotations for Super Bowls, Final Fours, and other major national events. In fact, the NFL already has awarded Super Bowl LII (2018) to Minneapolis, and the Final Four will be here in 2019.

STADIUM CAPACITY

66,655

The building is arguably the NFL's most stunning from the outside, all angles, smooth lines, and sparkling aesthetics. Rather than a retractable roof, which was deemed too

expensive to build, it has a lightweight, transparent one—the largest of its kind in North America—that bathes the field in natural light. Indeed, natural light is a primary theme here; the glazed entrances and glass-paneled walls of the stadium create oneness with the outdoor elements without the angry bite of freezing temperatures or punishing wind. It's all very green-friendly, and the seats are close in—the closest a mere 41 feet from the sideline.

ONLY HERE

Acoustically speaking, there are no two ways about it: The plan is for this to become known as football's loudest venue. One of the ideas behind the materials used and design implemented for the tilted roof was to "aim" the noise toward the visiting team's bench. The Metrodome was, if nothing else, capable of getting quite loud. This place should beat the Dome in that department, too.

MICHIE STADIUM
(WEST POINT, NEW YORK)

THERE ARE SOME things you must know before attending a football game at the home of the Black Knights of Army West Point. First, it's pronounced "Mikey" and named for the cadet who organized and coached Army's first football team in 1890 and later was killed during the Spanish-American War. Also, the

STADIUM CAPACITY
38,000

process of gaining admittance to campus, particularly on a crowded football Saturday, is a lengthy one; plan on at least an hour. And this is important: Go to the game, but stay for the humbling, inspirational experience of a day at West Point.

Michie Stadium is a proud structure—every little thing about it, just right—in a setting of solemnity and physical beauty. Overlooking the Hudson River, which snakes around West Point, and the Collegiate Gothic buildings of the campus, Michie is a place where a first-time visitor becomes lost in time. The stadium, though, is no relic; simple,

>> Hard against the Lusk Reservoir, Michie Stadium is an idyllic setting for football—and for the military pageantry that precedes every opening kickoff.

smart renovations over the years—to the playing surface, to the stands, to the exterior grounds—have made it better than ever. The bleachers rise lower on the east side of the stadium, offering views from the west stands of the Lusk Reservoir and the gorgeous greenery that surrounds it. This is, after all, Army. Everything about its wonderful football stadium was intricately planned.

ONLY HERE

Feel your heart swell during the Cadet March-On that begins 20 minutes before kickoff, with 1,000 cadets entering the field followed by the Army Band and a member of the Cadet Glee Club performing the national anthem. Ten minutes before kickoff, cadets jump from a helicopter and parachute onto the field. It's as good as any game.

» MCLANE STADIUM
(WACO, TEXAS)

AS BAYLOR UNIVERSITY entered the big-time with its formerly moribund football program, it took what was, on the surface, an antithetical approach to building a new stadium: It went even smaller (in terms of seating) than before. Whereas Floyd Casey Stadium, the Bears' home from 1950 to 2013, had a

STADIUM CAPACITY
45,000

capacity of 50,000—low by major-conference standards—McLane Stadium, opened for the 2014 campaign, seats 45,000, the fewest of any Big 12 building. Yet this has to be the swaggiest stadium in the Big 12, with its picturesque on-campus setting on the northern bank of the Brazos River and all the modern amenities. Not surprisingly, attendance has averaged above capacity—a stark change from so many down seasons at Floyd Casey.

A giant, high-def LED video board behind the open south end zone is the only thing disrupting views of "Lake Brazos," as it is known on campus, and the boats docked there

>> Baylor went small with McLane Stadium—and small is, in this case, way cool. Pound for pound, battles on the Brazos are as pleasing to the eye as any, anywhere.

that belong to those who arrive by water. Open concourses provide excellent views of the field below, and the concessions situation is almost too good to be true; there are approximately 250 concession points-of-sale in the new stadium, compared to about 50 at the old place. The new scoreboard is seven times the size of the old one, and the stadium square footage is twice at McLane what it was at Floyd Casey.

ONLY HERE

Before each home game, thousands of Baylor freshmen, donning gold football shirts with "Baylor Line" on the front and students' names—more often nicknames—on the back, race down a south-end ramp and across the field, where they form a human tunnel through which the Bears players run in from the north end. Then the students pile out through a tunnel and hustle up to the student section.

FARGODOME
(FARGO, NORTH DAKOTA)

ASK MINNESOTA, which in recent years has been beaten twice by North Dakota State University's football team. Ask Iowa State, Kansas, Kansas State, and Iowa, which likewise have been bested by NDSU. If a Football Bowl Subdivision (formerly called Division I-A) team plays the Football Championship Subdivision

STADIUM CAPACITY

19,000

(formerly called Division I-AA) Bison, it knows it's in for a gnarly fight. Perhaps needless to say, all such games are contested at the stadiums of the larger schools—because no big-league opponent would dare travel to the Fargodome to do battle with perhaps the greatest non-FBS program ever.

The Bison are the gold standard—Alabama, and then some—of the FCS ranks. They've won 13 national championships, and starting in 2011 they embarked on an amazing streak of five in a row. They play in the Missouri Valley Conference, because what says

>> Nowhere else in football do so few fans make so much noise—and the home team in Fargo tends to be pretty darned great. College football's big boys are too scared to go there, but you needn't be.

Missouri quite like snowy North Dakota? Yet it doesn't matter if the Peace Garden State is a bit of a misfit; the Fargodome can hang with any stadium, anywhere. This indoor, on-campus, 19,000-seat stadium is one of the loudest football venues in the country. Decibel levels compare with those of indoor stadiums in the NFL, but there's an extra edge to it all here; Bison games mean everything to fans in this area. Take in a game. You'll never look down your nose at the FCS again.

ONLY HERE

Bison football and the Fargodome are so cool, ESPN has held its national *College GameDay* show here—twice. Nowhere else in the lower-division ranks has this happened. The ESPN gang of Kirk Herbstreit, Lee Corso, et al., descended upon Fargo in 2013 and again one year later. Why? Because the Bison are great, but also because they'd had off-the-charts fun at the Fargodome the first time.

>> What? Your high school's stadium doesn't look like this? Suffice it to say, football—and prestige—are kind of important in Allen.

EAGLE STADIUM
(ALLEN, TEXAS)

FOLKS IN THE Lone Star State see their brand of high school football as being better—and bigger—than everyone else's. How else to explain the thinking behind the planning and construction of the publicly financed $60 million home of the Allen High School Eagles? When it opened in 2012, it was merely

STADIUM CAPACITY
18,000

the most expensive high school stadium known to man—but the powerhouse Eagles backed it up, winning three consecutive state championships. Structural issues forced the team to play elsewhere for the 2014 season, but the school district in affluent Allen, a northern suburb of Dallas, threw the necessary millions at the problem to restore the building to full health.

And what a robust venue it is, with seating for 18,000—9,000 on the home side, 5,000 on the visitor's side, and the rest a student section behind one end zone—and an

enormous parking lot that accommodates all the fans, not to mention an hours-long tailgating scene. Eagle Stadium is a horseshoe, with an open end that features an absolutely immense scoreboard–video board combo measuring 75 feet by 45 feet. There's also a three-tiered press box and, underneath the stands, a weight room most high school athletic directors would die for. Oh, and the next complaint about the Chick-fil-A and Texas barbecue concession stands will be the first.

ONLY HERE

A little over 7 miles north of Allen, McKinney (Texas) High School has its own project underway for a $70 million stadium that was scheduled for completion in 2017. Don't let anyone tell you the football rivalry between the schools wasn't the main driver behind this development. Yet there's another Texas town—Katy, outside Houston—that might top them both. Its stadium project, due for a 2017 completion, has been estimated to cost just north of $70 million.

MONUMENT VALLEY STADIUM
(MONUMENT VALLEY, UTAH)

IF EVER YOU WANT to take in a high school football environment that's different—in nearly every discernable way—from those driven by Friday-night hype and socioeconomic status, consider Monument Valley Stadium in the heart of Navajo Nation. The stands are small, but the views are endless at this reservation locale approximately 150 miles northeast of Grand Canyon National Park and within a whisker of Arizona's northern border. The Cougars of Monument Valley High School play there, squaring off against schools such as Navajo Pine, Whitehorse, and Rough Rock.

In this region of the Colorado Plateau, the low-rising stadium—frankly, its facades are almost nonexistent—is surrounded by the valley backdrop of sandstone buttes and sheer cliffs. It is awe inspiring, and it just might make you want to see America for a while

STADIUM CAPACITY
2,000

>> Go to the heart of Navajo Nation for football and an experience in Navajo culture in Monument Valley.

through the lens of the people here. There are fewer than 1,000 students at the high school, a majority of whom speak the language of the Navajo people, and one of them sings the national anthem—in Navajo—before every game. Try not to be emotionally moved by that! The concessions are charmingly simple, full of fry bread and beans and other sustenance that can only be considered the good stuff. Visitors are appreciated here, where mutual respect is a lovely thing.

ONLY HERE

Get your Navajo on by taking a Monument Valley day tour. See buttes, backcountry views, and petroglyphs in one of the most scenic parts of the country. Ride horses. Purchase pottery and other wares of the locals. Pro tip: If you drive your own vehicle, it'll need an epic washing by the time you're through. Well worth it.

STADIUM BOWL
(TACOMA, WASHINGTON)

CALL IT A CASTLE. Call it a meant-to-be hotel, which is what it was. But call Tacoma's Stadium High School—a French Renaissance–style building that towers above the shoreline— one of the most unique and picturesque public schoolhouses in our land, because that's exactly what it is. And the adjacent foot-

STADIUM CAPACITY

15,000

ball stadium, which sits downhill in a gulley overlooking Commencement Bay and the Puget Sound, more than completes the picture. Frederick Heath, the architect who built it, called then-Tacoma Stadium a "poem in masonry" and a "great athletic field set in the midst of superb natural scenery."

When it opened in 1910, the stadium held 11,000. The number increased to 32,000 as the stadium's significance grew—three US presidents spoke there—but now it's a more-perfect 15,000. The Stadium Bowl is home to both Stadium and Woodrow Wilson High

>> Stadium Bowl is a run-of-the-mill name for a setting that is anything but run-of-the-mill. Shouldn't all football vistas look like this one?

Schools, and the teams have a pretty strong rivalry. They aren't state powers, but they share a glorious, one-of-a-kind field, and that screams high school football in the best way. Things shut down for a while in 2016 when giant rains flooded the field, forcing both teams to scramble for places to play. All is good again, though, at this stadium that opens on the west end, offering views of the water that locals might take for granted. For the rest of us? It's must-see splendiferousness.

ONLY HERE

Five miles away from the Stadium Bowl along the shores of Commencement Bay sits Point Defiance Park, which includes a zoo, an aquarium, a botanical garden, beaches, hiking trails, and a boardwalk—this is one of those places you have to visit if you can. Rent a kayak and you'll be recommending this place to friends straight about.

≫ Who needs to watch the action on the field when the mother of all TVs is suspended over it? Cowboys fans can yell "Scoreboard!" at opposing fans regardless of who's winning.

≫ THE SCOREBOARD AT AT&T STADIUM (ARLINGTON, TEXAS)

WHEN BASKETBALL IS played here—an NBA All-Star Game, an NCAA Tournament Final Four, what have you—the scoreboard is larger than the court. When football is played at the palatial home of the NFL's Dallas Cowboys, it's merely larger than life. When "Jerry World" (nicknamed for Cowboys owner Jerry Jones) opened in 2009, Guinness World Records anointed the scoreboard the world's largest HD video display. It has since been surpassed, but this one is unique in that it's (1) indoors and (2) hangs over the field, as opposed to towering above an end zone; the resulting effect is that it looks so impossibly gigantic, it toys with the mind. A simple way to describe the scoreboard: It extends from one 20-yard line to the opposite 20-yard line. Unless our math is wrong, that's 60 yards—60!—of digital insanity. Fun fact: It has been hit more than once by punts. Wouldn't you love to see that?

>> If you're going to hang out in Buccaneer Cove during the game, be sure to get some boo—ahem. Make that *pirate's* booty.

THE PIRATE SHIP AT RAYMOND JAMES STADIUM (TAMPA)

LET'S START with the bad news: No, you cannot watch from the ship during a Tampa Bay Buccaneers game. Officially, access is limited to team personnel. But you certainly can hit a Bucs game and enjoy views of the extremely cool, 103-foot-long replica pirate ship that sits permanently "harbored" in Buccaneer Cove, in the north end zone of Raymond James Stadium. On-board cannons will fire seven times to signal a Bucs touchdown (pretty presumptuous, given the longer PATs in the NFL) and three times to announce a Bucs field goal. But stretch your legs and walk from your seat to Buccaneer Cove, too. When "Yo Ho (A Pirate's Life for Me)" blasts over the stadium's PA system, Bucs personnel on the ship will throw T-shirts, beads, and other booty to fans below. Is it cheesy? A little. But cheesy is fun if you allow it to be.

≫ Thirty-plus years after the installation of "the Blue," Boise State's field is arguably the most recognizable in all of college football.

THE BLUE TURF AT ALBERTSONS STADIUM (BOISE, IDAHO)

BOISE IS A beautiful place, a jewel of Treasure Valley, but the palette it's known best for is the simple, straightforward—yet absolutely jarring—blue of the field at Boise State University's football stadium. "The Blue," as locals call it, was installed in 1986, when the Broncos—a far cry from the success story they would become—competed in the Big Sky Conference. After the program ascended to the Football Bowls Subdivision ranks in 1996, and soon began establishing itself as a non-power-league powerhouse, the blue turf became perhaps the most talked-about playing surface in college football history. The NFL has a "Boise rule" that bans any playing surface that isn't green, but they don't call it the No Fun League for nothing. With their play, the Broncos have raised the bar for all FBS schools outside of the so-called Power 5 conferences. With their field, they raised it long ago.

≫ It's garish. It's glaring. It's . . . red? You'll never see another field like "the Inferno" at Roos.

THE RED TURF AT ROOS FIELD
[CHENEY, WASHINGTON]

EASTERN WASHINGTON University's football program hasn't broken into the big-time from the Big Sky Conference like Boise State did many years ago, but the Football Championship Subdivision Eagles have knocked off Oregon State and Washington State in recent seasons . . . on the road, of course. Yet it's at home at Roos Field, home of the red turf—"the Inferno," as it's known by locals—where one must see the pass-crazy Eagles play. The stadium seats a bit over 10,000 fans, and its red Sprinturf field is the only one of its kind. Some call the field ugly, but they're dead wrong. It's innovative and out of this world, and when the home team dons red uniforms and seemingly disappears into a sea of red, it's unlike anything else a first-time visitor has ever seen. The black end zones: a spectacular touch.

WALTER CAMP GATE AT THE YALE BOWL
(NEW HAVEN, CONNECTICUT)

IF YOU LOVE FOOTBALL—and you do—then you owe it to the "Father of American Football" to attend a game at the Yale Bowl and admire, and eventually walk through, the Walter Camp Memorial Gateway. It's a tribute to the man who did more to write the basic rules of football than anyone. Camp imagined such staples of the sport as the line of scrimmage, the four-down system, the 11-on-11 formation of play, and the yard markers on the field. He played and coached at Yale; as coach, he led a trio of national

≫ Outside the Yale Bowl stands a monument to a man without whom football never could've been all it has turned out to be. Walter Camp's portrait can be found at the National Portrait Gallery.

championship squads in 1888, 1891, and 1892. Later in life—as a sportswriter—Camp was the first to designate "All-America" teams, a tradition that bled into every other college sport. The Yale Bowl was built over 100 years ago, but Camp's presence is felt still. And, by the way, it's a great stadium—the largest by capacity in the Football Championship Subdivision ranks.

CHAPTER 4

SEATS . . . AND EATS

THE NFL OFTEN is accused of being a copycat league, with precious little originality among teams in the Xs-and-Os department. In the stands, though, each NFL game-day experience is different depending on where you are—and in the following five seating areas, it's one of a kind. Oh, and if you're one of those rare humans who likes to, you know, eat? Here are some of the league's best options for getting your grub on.

 Seats
- ► Hawks Nest, Seattle
- ► Dawg Pound, Cleveland
- ► Black Hole, Oakland
- ► Fanduelville, Jacksonville
- ► Lambeau Leap Zone, Green Bay

 Eats
- ► Pizza Box Nachos, Phoenix
- ► Texas Torta, Dallas
- ► Jumbo Pork Tenderloin, Indianapolis
- ► Anything from Primanti Bros., Pittsburgh
- ► The Kitchen Sink, East Rutherford, New Jersey

>> When the opponent is driving toward the north end zone, the game-long job of those in the Hawks Nest—to go absolutely bonkers—only intensifies.

>> HAWKS NEST
(CENTURYLINK FIELD, SEATTLE)

IF YOU LIKE your football environs raucous and uninhibited, the Hawks Nest is for you. If you can vibe off standing and stomping, shouting and screaming, drinking craft beer out of cans, and reveling nonstop for three-plus hours with 3,000 fans crammed into four sections of bleachers that rise in triangle formation to form the coolest-looking end-zone seating in football—again, still you. If you're thumbs-up to the down-and-dirty job of joining the loudest swath of fans in the consistently loudest stadium in NFL history, then by God you're home.

Clearly, the Hawks Nest isn't for just anybody. But if you're in your element at the intersection of hardy and party, then you will have one of the fan experiences of your life

FAQ

Are Hawks' Nest tickets hard to come by? Yes and no. Single-game tickets are sold out far in advance, but the prices on the secondary market are similar to those for upper-level seating at CenturyLink. It's a great value for the one-of-a-kind experience.

"sitting" there for a Seattle Seahawks game. There is no tougher place for an opponent to be than driving toward the north end zone in Seattle. That has much to do with the Seahawks' traditionally outstanding defenses, but the sheer volume of the "12th Man" crowd in Seattle has long created a dramatic home-field advantage. The heartbeat of the 12th Man is in the Hawks Nest.

The stands at CenturyLink are steep and hug tightly to the field throughout; those characteristics are pronounced in the Hawks Nest. Prepare for that part of the stadium to shake when the denizens get riled up. Which is pretty much always.

>> Win or lose, one thing is certain about the Pound: All mutts—the
mangier the better—are welcome.

>> DAWG POUND
[FIRSTENERGY STADIUM, CLEVELAND]

SINCE THE FRANCHISE reopened for business with a new stadium in 1999, the seats have been modern and comfy enough. Except for in the Dawg Pound. A larger (and slightly less authentic than it used to be) area of the stands, the Pound at FirstEnergy spans all sections—in two decks—behind the east end zone. It's old-style bleacher seating, and don't expect to do a whole lot of sitting. This is Party Central at Browns games; beery fans abound. And perhaps it's surprising (though it shouldn't be), but Pound tickets tend to go for more dough than those in other parts of the stadium that offer comparable, or better, sight lines. Still, this is Cleveland. These are the Browns. When

FAQ

Is barking mandatory?

Yeah, pretty much. Get used to chanting, "Here we go, Brownies, here we go—woof! woof!" It's a way of life, good home team or not, in the Dawg Pound. It stands for something. It's the anthem of a woebegone fan base, but there's a whole lot of virtue wrapped up in that. Get those vocal chords ready.

the team is bad, which it usually is, tickets are plentiful and less expensive than they are most everywhere else in the NFL.

But surely the Browns can hark back to the days of Otto Graham and Jim Brown and get good again. Or kind of? Seriously, Ohio is a great football state, full of knowledgeable fans, and Cleveland is one of the cities where the NFL was born. Strap on a snout or a muzzle, don a Browns jersey if it doesn't make you too depressed, and get a little crazy in the bleachers of the Pound.

SEATS

>> BLACK HOLE
(OAKLAND COLISEUM)

A **SPORTS ILLUSTRATED** story in 2016 dove into the Black Hole, chumming up to such lovely characters as Gorilla Rilla (think: ape in a top hat), Storm Raider (black skeleton mask, shades, spiked helmet), and Dr. Death (shoulder pads, wild hair, knife helmet). The eccentric epicenter of Raider Nation has claimed many other denizens of this sort: Voodoo Man, Skull Lady, the Oaktown Pirate. They're all, well, *nuts*. Who wouldn't want to share an afternoon—or, *shivers*, an evening—with them and their ilk?

They root hard in Section 105—behind the south end zone—of the Oakland Coliseum. Brace yourself, because it can get more than a little scary in there. Do yourself a favor

FAQ

Is the Black Hole really only Section 105? Well, it depends whom you ask. Most broadly defined, all ten 100-level sections behind the south end zone compose the Hole. But 105 is its heartbeat—the farther you are from it, the bigger a poser you are.

and don Raiders black, or at least neutral colors, because the next brawl in the Black Hole won't be the first (or the hundredth). Despite some inevitable troublemakers, most fans here are—like the nonfighting characters named above—simply fired up about the Raiders. They're also deeply concerned about the near future of the franchise: Will there be a move to Las Vegas? (By late winter of 2017, that loomed as a distinct possibility.) Will the Raiders move to another city? Or will they instead build a new stadium in the East Bay area? That would be a nice solution to the current stadium problems, which are profound.

>> Life is good on the pool deck in Jacksonville. Hey, why let the game get in the way of a wet-and-wild party?

>> FANDUELVILLE
(EVERBANK FIELD, JACKSONVILLE)

FORMERLY KNOWN AS the Clevelander Deck, the north end zone deck at the home of the NFL Jaguars is where one can find quite possibly the least attentive fans in football history. But that's no diss of North Florida. In all fairness, how up to speed on the action could anyone be whose head is underwater? That's what happens when you go to a football game and a pool party breaks out.

All fans at EverBank Field are allowed access to Fanduelville, which can accommodate up to 3,000 people. There are two swimming pools, multiple bars, gigantic videoboards, a DJ and dancing area, bikini-clad servers, and cabanas (with lounge furniture

FAQ

Are the cabanas open to everyone? In the central area of Fanduelville, yes; they are first-come, first-served. There are a limited number of VIP cabanas available for rental; they're off to both sides and can accommodate large groups.

and TVs) as far as the eye can see. If you're someone who likes to get up and move now and then during a three-plus-hour game, this is as fine and unique a spot to check out as there is in football. It's not uncommon for visitors to purchase cheap seats in the main stands and spend entire games in Fanduelville, which opens two hours prior to kickoff and stays open for two hours after the game is over. Bring a bathing suit. Better yet, wear one under your shorts and tank top. And if the mood should strike you, do something really crazy and—wait for it—fix your gaze on the field below and watch the game.

>> What better way to warm up on a frigid Green Bay evening than by mosh-pitting around a game-heated Packers touchdown-scorer?

LAMBEAU LEAP ZONE
(LAMBEAU FIELD, GREEN BAY)

THE GREAT Reggie White scooped up an Oakland Raiders fumble and, as he was being tackled, pitched the ball to safety LeRoy Butler, who raced 25 yards down the left sideline for a touchdown. Butler didn't stop running once he crossed the goal line; instead he pointed at the fans in the first row of the end zone stands to let them know he'd soon be joining their ranks, and then he leaped over the wall and into their arms. It was late December of 1993, the Packers were playoff bound for the first time in more than a decade—and the Lambeau Leap was born. Packers have celebrating touchdowns at home games in this manner ever since.

Aren't Packers tickets next to impossible to come by? Every game is a sellout, that's for sure, but end zone seats—even in the lowest rows—have been available on the secondary market for multiple games each season. A search of tickets to a late-2016 game revealed availability in Row 3 of one end zone for about $300— and in Row 1 of the opposite end zone for less than $200. Go figure.

It might seem like a long shot that you'll hit your first game at Lambeau and find a rejoicing Packer in your arms, but you'll never know unless you try. The official Leap Zone seats are in the first four rows of the end zone sections (101–106 and 133–138), and it's a mosh pit of would-be huggers after every Packers touchdown. If you're in Row 3 or 4 and a green-jerseyed player is headed your way, heave yourself wallward and go for it—not a bad way at all to get on *SportsCenter*. Regardless, these seats offer excellent views of arguably the best stadium in all of football.

... AND EATS

Menus change at stadiums all the time,
so get these while they're hot if you can:

Texas Torta (AT&T Stadium, Dallas Cowboys). Get the beef barbacoa, the pork carnitas, or the adobo chicken . . . hang on a second. Whoa, this Mexican sandwich actually comes packed with all three, along with refried beans, pico de gallo, and grilled onions. The bacon-wrapped fried jalapeño "garnish" is a nice touch.

Pizza Box Nachos (University of Phoenix Stadium, Arizona Cardinals). Pro tip: Don't even go there unless you're deadly serious about being fed. Crammed into a 12-inch pizza box—hello—they're topped with slow-roasted pork, chiles, olives, guacamole, sour cream, cheese sauce, and salsa, and did we mention the 12-inch pizza box?

Jumbo Pork Tenderloin (Lucas Oil Stadium, Indianapolis Colts). You want it because it's too big, perhaps by double, for the hearty, freshly baked bun on which it is served. Eating around the edges should keep you busy for a good quarter of football. Comes with excellent fries, too.

The Kitchen Sink (MetLife Stadium, New York Giants and New York Jets). Imagine not one, not two, but three hoagie rolls tested to their constitutional limits by a combo of chicken sausage, sweet Italian sausage, hot dogs, potatoes, banana peppers, onions, and—well, it's not called the Kitchen Sink for nothing. Good luck wrestling all that grub to the ground.

Anything from Primanti Bros. (Heinz Field, Pittsburgh Steelers). Because who doesn't want their sandwiches stuffed with french fries and coleslaw? Or mac-and-cheese and coleslaw? There are other ways to go, but get the capicola—it is what this Steel City institution is known best for.

CHAPTER 5

TAILGATING ...AND SAILGATING

MORE OFTEN THAN MOST football fans would care to admit, their favorite team's game doesn't live up to the full-bellied tailgating experience that preceded it. Never—ever—is that said in reverse, at least not by serious tailgaters. One can't control the weather, but hot/cold, sweaty/freezing, and rain-soaked/wind-battered merely are states of mind. The enjoyment of grilled meats and accompanying beverages is, on the other hand, an inalienable right of the American football fan.

 Tailgating
- ➤ Arrowhead Stadium, Kansas City
- ➤ New Era Field, Buffalo
- ➤ M&T Bank Stadium, Baltimore
- ➤ NRG Stadium, Houston
- ➤ FirstEnergy Stadium, Cleveland
- ➤ The Grove, Ole Miss
- ➤ Cockabooses, South Carolina
- ➤ House Parties, Wisconsin

 **Sailgating**
- ➤ At Tennessee
- ➤ At Washington

ARROWHEAD STADIUM
(KANSAS CITY, MISSOURI)

THE CHIEFS ARE nearly four decades removed from their last NFL championship season, yet they've been a prime contender for the league's tailgating title year after barbecue-sauce-stained year. What sets Arrowhead apart from everywhere else is, first and foremost, the number of fans who tailgate in the stadium parking lots; suffice it to say that going to a game without first logging several hours of pavement time borders on the unthinkable. Also, the festivities start extremely early; lots open four and a half hours prior to game time, and cars begin lining up outside the gates earlier than that.

>> There's no beating the tailgating at Arrowhead. Eat to your heart's content, and feel free to go heavy on the sauce. Barbecue sauce, that is.

And—goodness gracious—the food. Barbecue (Kansas City is famous for the quality and quantity of its sauces) and bacon are everywhere, and did we mention the bacon? It. Is. Everywhere. Be sure to prepay for parking through the Chiefs website—you'll save money and time at the tollbooth.

WHILE YOU'RE THERE

☑ Bacon gets wrapped around every food you can imagine here. Bring tons of it and, darn it, be an innovator.

☑ You've never seen so many footballs flying around in your life. Keep your head on a swivel at all times.

☑ Kaufman Stadium, home of the MLB Royals, sits directly across a big ol' parking lot from Arrowhead. Check it out whlle stretching your legs.

>> Buffalo reputedly has the hardest-partying tailgaters in the NFL. Note: Drinking oneself into a near-catatonic state is neither required nor advised.

>> NEW ERA FIELD
(ORCHARD PARK, NEW YORK)

THE BUFFALO BILLS aren't merely the only NFL franchise to suffer defeat in four consecutive Super Bowls. They're also the team with the reputedly drunkest fans in football. Winner, winner, buffalo chicken dinner! Um, kind of. Look, we're not here to glorify binge drinking. Nor should Bills fans bear the burden of representing beer- and booze-soaked tailgating-gone-wrong throughout the sport. Yet there's no doubt that imbibing—a lot—is as big a part of the tailgating culture here as it is anywhere. There are viral videos galore of Bills tailgaters breaking tables with body slams and other wrestling moves, and those are just the well-behaved ones. Hey, we kid. Oh, and buffalo

wings! This is, of course, the spiritual homeland of these culinary delights and gastrointestinal rabble-rousers. Ingest them by the plateful. Drink, if you're so inclined. But maybe don't play Dizzy Bats. (Trust us on this.)

WHILE YOU'RE THERE

Find "Pinto Ron," the Bills tailgater who grills meat on the hood of his impossibly old Ford Pinto and cooks wings in a (huh?) mailbox. No, really.

If you prefer a watered-down version of this particular experience — or can't deal with the cold — you can tailgate indoors at Club Buffalo Bills in the ADPRO Sports Training Center. It's kid-friendly and has some great interactive areas, including one where you can attempt field goals.

M&T BANK STADIUM
(BALTIMORE)

STEP 1: Get your car parked wherever. Step 2: Lock your shyness in the trunk and introduce yourself to as many Ravens Roost tailgating groups (there are dozens, identifiable by number) as you can find. Not all Ravens Roosts welcome outsiders, but most of them do, especially if you arrive with good food (hint: crab cakes) and/or drink (hint: local craft brews) to share. Fans here have strong tailgating game, sharply honed over the five—five!—hours lots are open before every game. Prepare to lose at cornhole. Prepare to embarrass, and just maybe thrill, yourself in a dance-off inspired by former Ravens su-

>> Spend a few—or even five—hours amid Ravens fans before the game, and you'll see tailgating done at an extraordinarily high level. And you can take that to the M&T Bank.

perstar linebacker Ray Lewis's famous pregame introductions. And prepare to be impressed by tailgating done exceptionally well. One more thing: Wear purple and black. It seems to have a way of ingratiating a visitor to the masses here.

WHILE YOU'RE THERE

☑ **Be sure to check out RavensWalk, in between lots B and C, which has bars, food booths, and live music. It opens three hours before kickoff.**

☑ **Visit the National Aquarium in the Inner Harbor area of the city, just over a 1-mile walk from the stadium.**

☑ **Dine on crab cakes while in Charm City. Once you're finished, dine on more crab cakes. Rinse, repeat.**

≫ Three words, people: Pass the brisket. And if you should find yourself being hoisted in the air like this guy, please be careful.

≫ NRG STADIUM (HOUSTON)

EVERYTHING IS BIGGER in Texas, right? That happens to include the set of rules and restrictions on tailgating in stadium lots before Texans games, so be sure to read up on the team's website before planning your visit. (Know this: You'll want to prepurchase hangtags for your parking spot and, if you're bringing one, your barbecue grill.) But once situated, you'll be surrounded by a massive display of BBQ of the highest order. The brisket here? It's the gold standard. The pork spareribs are another staple of the Southeast Texas menu, as are an unfathomably delicious array of sausages, some of

them with Cajun influences. If you're picking up a "meat" vibe, it's because Texans tailgaters prize meat with as much high-and-tight discipline as any running back who has ever carried a pigskin. If you're cooking here, you'd better bring your A-game.

WHILE YOU'RE THERE

☑ **Have we mentioned the grilled crabs and crawfish? They're at Texans tailgates, too. Find some.**

☑ **It's called Space Center Houston, and it's the closest you'll ever come to being a NASA astronaut. To visit the city and not get your outer space on is a tragic move.**

☑ **Spend a day on Galveston Island. The Gulf of Mexico beaches are less than an hour away.**

FIRSTENERGY STADIUM
(CLEVELAND)

WE CAN ALL AGREE on this: The Cleveland Browns aren't always particularly great at playing football. More than occasionally—and we can all agree on this, too—they're state-of-the-art terrible. But let's not turn this into a same-old, same-old tear-down of the Browns, OK? Their tailgating fans deserve too much love for that, and besides—Beer Can Chicken, anyone? If there's a single greatest tailgating innovation out there, it's Beer Can Chicken. In short, it's a chicken filled with beer and then grilled. At its full, glorious length, it's a chicken filled with beer and then grilled. Do you feel the magic

>> Beer Can Chicken, but can chicken beer? Think about that while you dine on—wait for it—chicken and beer.

that's happening here? Pick your dry rub, but understand that this boils down to chicken and beer, beer and chicken—as long as you're willing to yank out the giblets, you almost can't go wrong. And then the game will happen, which might not go so well.

WHILE YOU'RE THERE

☑ The Rock and Roll Hall of Fame and Museum, on the Lake Erie shore in downtown Cleveland, is a must-see. Less than half a mile from the stadium, it's open seven days a week. It's an incredible building, architecturally, with exhibits inside on rock and roll, gospel, blues, folk, country—something for absolutely everybody.

THE GROVE
(OXFORD, MISSISSIPPI)

BEFORE ANYTHING ELSE, understand two things: The University of Mississippi is always to be called Ole Miss, and the Grove is at the very top of most lists of the best tailgates in college football. Named for its gloriously abundant array of trees—which includes a dozen or more species of oaks alone—the Grove is a 10-acre plot in the middle of campus and a roughly half-mile walk to Vaught-Hemingway Stadium. Fans gather here by the tens of thousands on game days, with estimates reaching as high as 100,000. Many tailgaters, especially students, dress in their Sunday best; you'll see young men in slacks and bow ties, and young women in sundresses and heels. Food generally falls into

> For most fans—especially the younger ones—attending a Rebels game without starting the day at the Grove is simply unthinkable. It is indeed the place to be.

two categories: Southern-style hors d'oeuvres and, of course, barbecue. A truly special ritual is the Walk of Champions, when the team parades through the center of the Grove on the way to the stadium.

WHILE YOU'RE THERE

☑ **Rebels fans are famous for their "Hotty Toddy" cheer. It'll begin with an "Are you ready?" called from somewhere in your midst. Your callback: "Hell, yes! Damn right!" And then the cheer:**

Hotty Toddy, gosh almighty
Who the hell are we? Hey!
Flim Flam, Bim Bam
Ole Miss, by damn!

» Cockabooses aren't the only way to tailgate at South Carolina, but it's sure worth poking around them to see how the well-heeled fans do it. Wouldn't it be a kick to own one?

» COCKABOOSES
(COLUMBIA, SOUTH CAROLINA)

THE UNIVERSITY OF South Carolina might be the most underrated tailgating school in the country. Here, you'll find the Cockabooses—22 train cabooses, all painted in bold garnet, on an otherwise unused railroad spur on the southeast side of Williams-Brice Stadium. They are privately owned, 270-square-foot train cars, uniform in appearance on the outside but decorated in fascinatingly different ways by owners on the inside, and equipped with kitchens, bathrooms, A/C, heat—this is luxury. You might not be invited to party in one, but you sure can ask to have a look-see. In any event, you don't have to own a Cockaboose to tailgate in style here. Gamecock Park is the main tailgating

area, a state-of-the-art 50-acre expanse, lined with scarlet oaks, that includes parking for over 3,000 vehicles on a first-come, first-served basis. It has cable television hookups, electrical outlets, and permanent restrooms and opens at 8 a.m. or five hours before kickoff, whichever is later.

WHILE YOU'RE THERE

☑ Less than a half mile from the stadium, on the west side of Assembly Street, is the Capital City Stadium lot. It's inexpensive (only $10 in 2016) to park there and perfect if you plan to "tailgate" on foot.

☑ Make sure you're in Gamecock Park for the team's pregame walk through Garnet Way. It's a lovely spectacle.

☑ Remember, you're less than a two-hour drive from the Atlantic Ocean. Day trip!

>> If it's been a few years—or decades—since you last attended a keg party, you're overdue. You might want to brush up on your beer pong skills.

>> HOUSE PARTIES
(MADISON, WISCONSIN)

YOU WILL NOT drive all the way to Camp Randall Stadium at the University of Wisconsin. You will not even try. The author happens to be an alumnus, and he can assure you it's not even a little bit worth it. Yet Madtown is one of the great tailgating towns in our fair land, of that you can be sure. It's just that the game is played a little differently here. Park in lots and on side streets many blocks away, and from there join the mass of red-clad humanity on foot. If it's cold, don't be a baby. A bratwurst or three cooked in beer will warm you up, and then there's the aforementioned beer—it's the primary food source here. Badgers fans gather in Regent Street bars, but that's too easy. The house

parties all around Camp Randall, which sits in a residential neighborhood, are more than plentiful and generally open to anyone who's willing to pay a few bucks for a plastic cup. The keg: It's on the front lawn.

WHILE YOU'RE THERE

☑ State Street—extending from campus to the state capitol—is one of the most eclectic walks in America. Eat, drink, and shop for Badgers gear, bongs, and anything and everything else.

☑ If it's (very) early in the season and still summery, sit outside on the Memorial Union Terrace. The shores of Lake Mendota are beautiful, the locally crafted beer delicious, and the people-watching sublime.

☑ Mickies Dairy Bar on Monroe Street, in the shadows of Camp Randall, is a 1950s-style diner that cannot be missed.

SAILGATING

The University of Tennessee and the University of Washington have had fans arriving by boat since the 1960s. But these are no dock-and-go operations; they're full-fledged tailgates on water. Or should we say, sailgates. A tale of the tape:

TENNESSEE & WASHINGTON

☑ Body of water

The Tennessee River near Knoxville is scenic enough, though your breath won't be taken away. What's cooler than all get-out is how far some boats travel along the Tennessee to get there.	Lake Union provides views of the Cascade Mountains to the east and the Olympic Mountains to the west. Breath: gone.

☑ How to do it

Vol Navy Cruises offers inexpensive passage; book your reservations far in advance.	Take one of the chartered boats run by a local restaurant. It'll be pricier, but you'll stuff yourself full of seafood and drink and be thrilled you did.

☑ When to do it

September is the ideal time. Early October works, too. After that, it gets pretty cold.	It's Seattle—pack rain gear and an extra layer and don't worry about what you can't control.

☑ Once you get there

Volunteer Landing is a couple of miles from Neyland Stadium, but there's lots to do there before you start hoofing it along the riverfront path. It's a real party.	Husky Harbor is much closer to Husky Stadium. Stay on your craft as long as you can; once moored, there's not much else to do than go to the game.

☑ The stadiums

Neyland Stadium is a bucket-list destination for its sheer size and the inimitable quality of a Southeastern Conference game-day experience. Don't do this on a nonconference weekend unless the opponent is big-time.	Husky Stadium is a bucket-list destination because of its stirring beauty both inside and out. There isn't a more glorious setting in college football.

≫ Stop us if you can think of a more pleasant way to eat and drink
pregame than by luxuriating on a boat. We didn't think so.

CHAPTER 6

RITES OF PASSAGE

>>

STEP OUTSIDE YOUR personal sphere of fandom if you dare and pretend, for a freeing moment—or 10 such moments—that you root for one of the teams in this chapter. It isn't so hard; you just have to try a little. The rewards will be towels and flags, a rainbow of roses, and, um, toilet paper. Don't worry, it's better than it sounds.

 Rites of Passage

>> Any self-respecting Yinzer has a Terrible Towel and isn't afraid to wave it. It wouldn't be a Steelers game without the gold standard of rally props.

TERRIBLE TOWELS
(PITTSBURGH)

BY NOW, we've all seen enough sports crowds waving "rally towels" at games that the act might not seem very original. Oh, but it's an original, all right—a Steel City original, Yinzer to the core. The Terrible Towel tradition was championed in 1975 by the late Myron Cope, Pittsburgh native and longtime Steelers radio color analyst, as the team was on its way to a second straight Super Bowl title. To this day, it is waved at Heinz Field—as needed for rallies, and more formally at designated times of each game—by every Steelers fan with a pulse. Good luck finding a Yinzer who doesn't have a Terrible Towel or 17 lying about the abode. They're easy to shop for, but be sure to buy an official one; since 1996, millions of dollars in proceeds have gone to a local school that provides care for people with intellectual and physical disabilities.

>> When the flag is raised, fans of the Seahawks erupt—it is their call to duty. Supporting the home team here is serious business.

12TH MAN FLAG [SEATTLE]

TO ATTEND a Seahawks game (as a non–visiting team's fan) at Seattle's Century-Link Field is to take on a certain degree of responsibility. Here, in the ear-splitting-volume capital of the NFL, the home fans are known as the 12th Man—and their full-throated contribution to the cause is so revered, the organization long ago retired No. 12 in their honor. Behind the south end zone prior to the opening kickoff of each game, an enormous "12" flag is raised up a towering pole. It's a ritual that, if you've never seen it before—or even if you have—will send chills down your spine. In that moment, it is your duty to summon a level of noise from the depths of your gut that you may not have realized you were capable of making. You'll never again see 12 as just another number.

>> Join the Revolution—even for just one Sunday. And, no, Tom Brady's career doesn't date back to the 1800s.

>> END ZONE MILITIA
(FOXBOROUGH, MASSACHUSETTS)

THE WORD *militia* is pretty loaded in America nowadays. (For that matter, *patriot* is, too.) Yet all associations with the term can be checked at the doors of Gillette Stadium prior to New England Patriots games. Tom Brady may be the field general to end all field generals, and the man he reports to—Bill Belichick—is hailed as one of football's great leaders of men. Yet the 20 or so Revolutionary War reenactors who compose the End Zone Militia do the sort of grunt work that makes this a one-of-a-kind place to see a game regardless of the final score. When the Patriots score, 1800s-style muskets are fired into the air with true brilliance. If you sit near either end zone, the smell of gun smoke will waft your way and perhaps transport you to another era in our nation's history. If that's too dramatic for you, sorry—you're not militia material.

>> It's a hallowed tradition of the highest order: the heaving of
toilet paper. Roll Tide? Never. Rolls of two-ply? Always.

ROLLING OF TOOMER'S CORNER
(AUBURN, ALABAMA)

WHAT'S A CELEBRATION without toilet paper, anyway? Ever since Auburn's 1972 Iron Bowl victory over unbeaten Alabama—before which Tigers halfback Terry Henley promised his team would "beat the No. 2" out of the Crimson Tide—fans here have celebrated wins by festooning a pair of oak trees that loom above the intersection of Magnolia Avenue and College Street, site of Toomer's Drug Store for over 100 years, with copious rolls of the good stuff. (Single-ply? For amateurs.) The tradition was halted after the 2010 Iron Bowl, in which Cam Newton led an amazing comeback en route to an Auburn national championship. A Dadeville, Alabama, man, Harvey Updyke Jr.—a misguided Tide supporter—poisoned the trees; too sick to save, they finally were cut down in 2013. But they were replaced by two towering live oaks in 2015, and the "No. 2" tradition in football was reborn. Go on, take a three-step drop and let a roll fly.

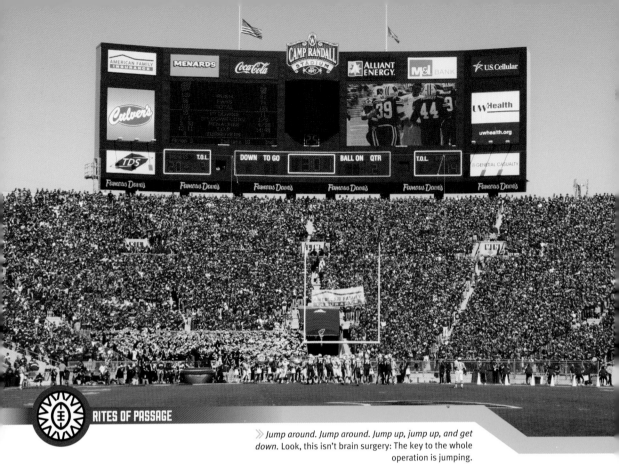

>> *Jump around. Jump around. Jump up, jump up, and get down.* Look, this isn't brain surgery: The key to the whole operation is jumping.

>> "JUMP AROUND"
(MADISON, WISCONSIN)

IT HAPPENS LIKE CLOCKWORK: As the start of the fourth quarter nears at a University of Wisconsin home game, journalists covering the visiting team suddenly begin tweeting cries for help and farewells to the world. That's because "Jump Around" is booming in over the loudspeakers at Camp Randall Stadium, fans of the Badgers are quite literally "Jump! Jump! Jump!"-ing, and the stands are swaying and shaking to such an extent that it feels as if the entire edifice will collapse at any moment. (Other than that, it isn't scary at all.) The rite originated in Camp Randall's huge student section—dive into the sea of about 15,000 who sit in Sections J through P if you can, even if it's only to "Jump"—but most everyone else who is able-bodied enough to participate does so nowadays. It's fun and seemingly never fails to give the Badgers a boost on the field.

ANIMATION

>> It isn't always easy to crawl out of bed early on New Year's Day, but the Rose Parade is worth it. Float on over.

THE ROSE PARADE
(PASADENA, CALIFORNIA)

IF YOU'RE BATTLING a New Year's Eve hangover, suck it up. If you're in Southern California and holding a ticket to the Rose Bowl game, strap in for an extra-long day— there's something very wrong about being there, yet taking a pass on the Rose Parade. It's an event that stands on its own, by the way, in case you *aren't* going to the game, but the Rose Parade–Rose Bowl marriage is, as football experiences go, made in heaven. A 5.5-mile procession of marching bands, equestrian units, spectacular floats, and floral magnificence lasts, from start to finish, only about two hours. Every New Year's Day (or Monday, January 2, if the holiday falls on a Sunday) in Pasadena, hundreds of thousands line the streets as the parade travels north on South Orange Grove Boulevard to Colorado Boulevard—a great spot, where the major television networks are set up—and east from there to Sierra Madre Boulevard, then north to Paloma Street near Victory Park. All of it: gorgeous and splendid.

≫ Calling someone a hog isn't very nice. Calling the Hogs is quite a different story. In Arkansas, it's as friendly a gesture as one can make.

CALLING THE HOGS
(FAYETTEVILLE, ARKANSAS)

WE COULD ARGUE all day about the most eloquent three words ever spoken. *Love thy neighbor. Et tu, Brute? E = MC²*. But no—it's totally *Woo Pig! Sooie!* If you encounter a passel of Arkansas Razorbacks fans at a diner, in an airport, or on the street, then the time for a Hog Call has come. If you're among 70,000 of them at Razorback Stadium, all the better. But let's cut straight to how you do it. With arms raised and fingers wiggling, prepare for upward of 10 seconds of "Woooooooo," with the volume rising throughout. Next, bring your arms down and clench your hands into fists for the "Pig!" And then—as though your very life depends on it—thrust a single fist into the air for the "Sooie!" Yet you're not finished: This must be repeated twice (a total of three times, if you're scoring at home) before a final shout of "Razorbacks!" Your fine work will be done.

≫ Clemson games are lit from the moment Tigers players—and, here, coach Dabo Swinney—rub the rock. From there, it's down the hill and into the fray.

≫ RUBBING HOWARD'S ROCK
(CLEMSON, SOUTH CAROLINA)

CLEMSON BILLS IT as the "most exciting 25 seconds in all of college football," and it is indeed a hair-raiser. But first, the Tigers walk out of their locker room in the west end of Memorial Stadium—and out of the stadium altogether—and board buses that drive them around to the east end. They then walk through a gate and up a tunnel to the field. A cannon blasts, and the players rub the rock and race down a hill and onto a field known as Death Valley. Howard's Rock, a large chunk of white flint, dates to the 1960s, when a friend brought it from Death Valley, California, to then-coach Frank Howard. As the story goes, Howard told his players, "If you're going to give me 100 percent, you can rub that rock. If you're not, keep your filthy hands off it." Watch the ritual at a Clemson game—it'll fire you up big-time.

>> Ralphie—she sure is a beauty. And the handlers who race her around Folsom Field darn sure are athletes.

>> # RALPHIE'S RUN
(BOULDER, COLORADO)

BEFORE EACH GAME at the University of Colorado's Folsom Field, and again before the second half, Ralphie, the school's live buffalo mascot, leads the team out of an end zone tunnel and does a full sprint up one sideline, across the opposite end zone, and back down the other sideline. Led by Ralphie Handlers—students who train, and are recognized, as athletes by the school—this heck of a guy is a sight to behold. Only it's not a guy; Ralphie V is a female, as each of her predecessors was, because female buffaloes are smaller and less temperamental than males. To this point, each Ralphie has served as mascot for about a decade. (The life expectancy of buffaloes in captivity is approximately 25 years.) When Ralphie is led out of her trailer and into a pen situated just outside the tunnel, everyone in attendance braces for one of college football's most captivating half minutes.

>> Not that anyone needs a reason to wish to travel to Hawaii, but there's something extra special about the Haka as performed by the Rainbow Warriors.

>> THE HAKA
(HONOLULU, HAWAII)

A WHILE BACK, it was determined that the University of Hawaii football team should not perform its ritual Haka dance while the opposing team is on the field. It's a shame, because nothing is more dramatic than the Haka done with an ocean of players, eyes wild, tongues out, facing—and intimidating—the other squad. It's a war cry that originated with the Maori people of New Zealand and was made famous by that country's All Blacks national rugby team. Hawaii's Rainbow Warriors brought it into the college football realm in 2006, the first of a number of American teams that have performed the Haka in recent years. Nowadays, it's a ritual that is seen pregame—after the opposing squad has retreated to its locker room—only. But it'll still raise the hairs on your arms. Such emotion; such passion. And if you can see it in Honolulu, lucky you.

CHAPTER 7

JUST DO IT

SOME OF THE ACTIVITIES in this chapter come with heavy-duty price tags. A couple of others might cost you merely a shred or two of your dignity. Regrets? Let's hope there aren't any at all. Go to a championship game. Spend a football weekend picking winners (fingers crossed!) in Vegas. Take your shot at coaching. Why the heck not? Just do it.

 Just Do It
- ➤ Go to a Super Bowl
- ➤ Go to the Pro Bowl
- ➤ Go to the NFL Draft
- ➤ Go to the College Football Playoff
- ➤ Spend a Weekend in a Las Vegas Sports Book
- ➤ Take a Gatorade Shower
- ➤ Play Fantasy Football
- ➤ Do the Punt, Pass & Kick
- ➤ Do It Yourself: The Combine
- ➤ Coach a Youth Football Team

GO TO A SUPER BOWL

LET'S ASSUME, just for the sake of argument, that you aren't made of money. (If we're way off on that, we sincerely apologize.) Procuring tickets to a Super Bowl isn't going to be easy. This is the mother of all football games, and it's the hardest ticket to score by conventional methods. Understand this: There is no direct way for the public to purchase tickets. It just doesn't exist. Things have changed a wee bit since the first Super Bowl, when face-value seats were available for—wait for it—under $10.

If you're an NFL season-ticket holder, you have a shot at tickets—if your team makes the Super Bowl, that is—through the team's lottery system. (The longer you've held those season tickets, the better your odds of being rewarded.) Everyone else must apply for entrance into the NFL's lottery, which is a long shot. Do it every year, though, because the thousands of names drawn get to pay face value. Realistically, what you'll likely have to do is suck it up and either buy tickets on the secondary market (they will be at least

» Winning a Super Bowl, as the Denver Broncos did to cap the 2015 season, is cause for a huge celebration. Just getting there—as a fan—is cause to celebrate, too.

$1,000 a pop for the upper sections) or, if you're shrewd and daring, travel to the Super Bowl city and buy in-person from a fellow citizen. Look, this is the Super Bowl—the ultimate bucket-list experience. You're going to have to pay for it.

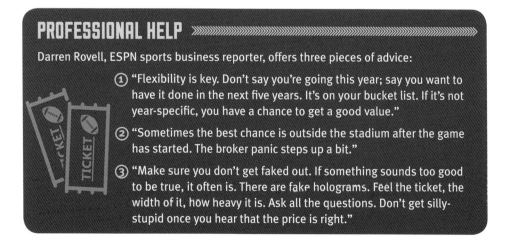

PROFESSIONAL HELP »»»»»»»»»»»»»»»»»»»»»»»»»

Darren Rovell, ESPN sports business reporter, offers three pieces of advice:

① "Flexibility is key. Don't say you're going this year; say you want to have it done in the next five years. It's on your bucket list. If it's not year-specific, you have a chance to get a good value."

② "Sometimes the best chance is outside the stadium after the game has started. The broker panic steps up a bit."

③ "Make sure you don't get faked out. If something sounds too good to be true, it often is. There are fake holograms. Feel the ticket, the width of it, how heavy it is. Ask all the questions. Don't get silly-stupid once you hear that the price is right."

JUST DO IT

GO TO THE PRO BOWL

THE PRO BOWL got rather ridiculous in its last few years at Aloha Stadium in Honolulu. The ill-conceived blending of American Football Conference and National Football Conference players into each team eroded an essential value of any all-star game, which is to pit players from one half of the league against players from the other. The level of competitiveness on the field dropped noticeably. If attendance at Aloha Stadium didn't markedly wane, television ratings did. So the NFL did a couple of really smart things: It moved the Pro Bowl to Orlando and restored the AFC vs. NFC format.

News flash: Orlando is easier to get to for most NFL fans than Honolulu. Camping World Stadium, a 65,000-seat venue that underwent $200 million in renovations to help score the Pro Bowl, also happens to be quite a bit nattier than Aloha Stadium. You'll be a bit farther from the beaches of Oahu, but guess what? As of late 2016, lower-bowl seats near the 50-yard line for the January 2017 Pro Bowl were going, on the online market, for about $200. This is a highly affordable excursion with many ancillary enticements.

There's a fan fest at the ESPN Wide World of Sports Complex at Walt Disney World Resort where you can watch Pro Bowl practices. Also: a Pro Bowl–themed 5K run and a parade of players in the Magic Kingdom.

PROFESSIONAL HELP ▶▶▶

Amy Sweezey, meteorologist for WESH 2 in Orlando, offers the following insight on the weather: "Around the time of the Pro Bowl, Central Florida is smack-dab in the middle of dry season. Those afternoon summer thunderstorms for which we're so famous are distant memories all winter long. Our average high temperature in Orlando in January is 72, and the average low is 50. This is when we call our friends to the north and brag about our Sunshine State. We've had occasional freezes around this time, but Orlando usually still warms quickly by afternoon thanks to our winter sun."

GO TO THE NFL DRAFT

FROM 1965 UNTIL 2014, the NFL Draft was in New York City. No doubt, that added all kinds of luster to the event from a fan-participation standpoint—especially during the Radio City Music Hall years of 2006 to 2014. But the draft has since moved out of New York, to Chicago in 2015 and 2016 and to Philadelphia in 2017; future sites will be determined on a yearly basis. One way to look at it is that you now can pick a draft to attend based on geographical convenience. Go to the draft anywhere, and you'll see every jersey in the NFL on the backs of attendees. This has to be the only event in football where that can be said. The Pro Bowl might come close, but only the draft has someone from *everywhere*.

Typically, this has not been a cost-prohibitive event to attend. And it really is fun, if you're just nutty enough about the NFL to enjoy this sort of thing. There will be countless hours to while away—Round 1 is on Thursday night, Rounds 2 and 3 on Friday, and

>> For draftniks, months of waiting come to a boil as NFL teams finally
make their selections. It's a one-of-a-kind spectacle.

Rounds 4 through 7 on Saturday—and only diehards take in all of the above. This is, at the highest order, about representing your team. If there's no one there to cheer—or boo—your team's top pick, it's embarrassing.

GOOD TO KNOW >>>>>>>>>>>>>>>>>>>>>>>>>>>>>>>>>>

Three pieces of intel from those who've been there:

① NFL commissioner Roger Goodell will be booed as he strides to the podium to announce first-round picks. This seems to be a stone-cold lock.

② Make friends with fans from all around the league. You never know when you'll need your next hookup for game tickets.

③ It's a great place to meet—and take selfies with—NFL luminaries. With so much downtime, these guys are very reach-out-and-touchable.

GO TO THE COLLEGE FOOTBALL PLAYOFF

PERHAPS THE BEST THING about the break from the previous championship format—the Bowl Championship Series—is that additional destinations and venues have been brought into the College Football Playoff fold. The 2017 season semifinals venues: the Rose Bowl in Pasadena, California, and the Sugar Bowl in New Orleans—traditional championship sites—with the title game in Atlanta's spanking-new Mercedes-Benz Stadium. The 2018 season semis: Arlington, Texas, and Miami Gardens, Florida, with the title game in Santa Clara, California. The 2019 semis: Atlanta and Glendale, Arizona, with the title game in New Orleans. If you aren't allegiant to a particular college football superpower, just pick where you'd like to go and plan accordingly.

Huge college games are, in many ways, better than anything else in football, including the NFL. The passion and pageantry of the college game at its highest level exists on its own plane. You'll find essentially half the stands bathed in one team's colors,

>> The 2016 season came to a crescendo with a championship game for the ages. Alabama receiver ArDarius Stewart (above) helped get his team off to a strong start, but Clemson quarterback Deshaun Watson (left) proved too good to be stopped. Final score: Tigers 35, Tide 31.

and half the stands bathed in the other's. And the clashes of conferences—of regions of America—can be outrageously palpable. The South vs. the North? It doesn't exist in any meaningful way in the NFL, but it sure does in college football.

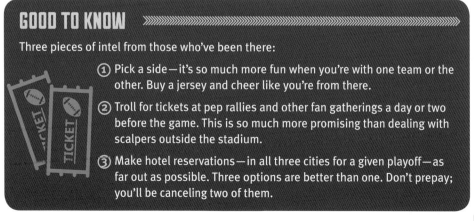

GOOD TO KNOW

Three pieces of intel from those who've been there:

① Pick a side—it's so much more fun when you're with one team or the other. Buy a jersey and cheer like you're from there.

② Troll for tickets at pep rallies and other fan gatherings a day or two before the game. This is so much more promising than dealing with scalpers outside the stadium.

③ Make hotel reservations—in all three cities for a given playoff—as far out as possible. Three options are better than one. Don't prepay; you'll be canceling two of them.

» Plunk a wad of bills onto the counter and watch games with the exciting edge of having a real stake in the action. But first, study the board—this is one book you won't fall asleep reading.

SPEND A WEEKEND IN A LAS VEGAS SPORTS BOOK

THERE ARE COUNTLESS things to do in Sin City—see comedy and magic shows, soak in sun amidst beautiful people at resort pools, gamble at the tables—but there's nothing like the experience of spending a good 12 hours on Saturday followed by the same on Sunday in a top-of-the-line sports book. It very likely will liquor you up and leave you hanging out to dry. Yet it's oh so fun, not to mention perfectly legal.

All the Vegas hotels with serious sports books take reservations; in the Caesars Palace book on a football Saturday or Sunday in 2016, for example, $100 got you a comfy leather chair that was yours for the entire day ($300 got you a seat—and all drinks on the house—in the VIP section). But most books have one or more nearby video poker bars; grab a stool at one and, as long as your machine is active (pro tip: play slowwwly), you can drink for free. Meanwhile, get your sports wagers in early—needless to say, lines get

longer right before kickoffs of games—and, for goodness sake, don't chase your losses and dig yourself into a big hole. It's fun enough to have small action on a slew of games.

PROFESSIONAL HELP »»»»»»»»»»»»»»

Ryan Kijewski, supervisor at Caesars Palace Race and Sports Book in Las Vegas, offers three pieces of advice:

① "With new bettors, if you're unsure about anything, always ask. We have pretty savvy and veteran sports ticket-writers, and they're more than happy to answer any question a guest has."

② "A 10-team parlay is what I like to refer to as a 'lotto ticket.' Two- or three-team parlays are smarter bets."

③ "A common mistake is walking away from the window without actually looking at your ticket and realizing you chose the wrong side by accident."

» Now that's teamwork: Ezekiel Elliott distracted Urban Meyer just as a celebratory wave approached the Ohio State coach. And Clemson's Dabo Swinney gets drenched to the right.

TAKE A GATORADE SHOWER

FORMER NFL COACH Bill Parcells was known as a grumpy, temperamental sort, which makes it rather hilarious that he was the central figure—the dumpee, if you will—in the rise of the Gatorade shower. It was the 1986 season, when the New York Giants won 14 regular-season games, and three more in the postseason, to become champions. Seventeen—that's how many victories were punctuated by a giant jug of the cold, colorful stuff being emptied onto the head and shoulders of Parcells. An iconic tradition was born, though typically Gatorade showers are reserved for victories of special significance. A title game. The defeat of a bitter rival. Occasionally, even, one of those wins that comes at the best of all possible times for a coach whose employment is in jeopardy.

So now: you. Why on earth would you—in all probability, not an NFL or even a college head coach—submit yourself to such ice-cold treatment? For the very same reason we suggest all things in this book: to have been there and done that. Technically, it's probably OK to substitute a different brand of sports drink and even, if you can live with

yourself, a giant bucket that isn't orange in color. The element of surprise would seem to be a key to the whole operation, though you'll have to be pretty inventive to allow that part to happen.

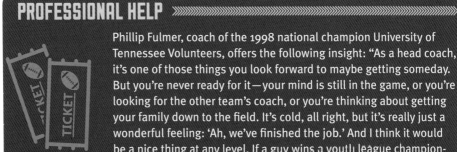

PROFESSIONAL HELP ➤➤➤➤➤➤➤➤➤➤➤➤➤➤➤➤

Phillip Fulmer, coach of the 1998 national champion University of Tennessee Volunteers, offers the following insight: "As a head coach, it's one of those things you look forward to maybe getting someday. But you're never ready for it—your mind is still in the game, or you're looking for the other team's coach, or you're thinking about getting your family down to the field. It's cold, all right, but it's really just a wonderful feeling: 'Ah, we've finished the job.' And I think it would be a nice thing at any level. If a guy wins a youth league champion-ship and the kids are really into it, why not?"

JUST DO IT

≫ OK, so fantasy football is a step or two removed from "real" football, but so what? Grab the controls of your team and see where you can take it.

PLAY FANTASY FOOTBALL

ARE YOU REALLY that person who has been holding out on this expression of football-fan geekdom? Actually, you're not alone. You're in league with millions of football fans who missed the fantasy train as the activity grew in popularity over the past 20 years, and chances are you missed it on purpose. Maybe your idea of a "fantasy" just plain doesn't involve football. (That would be so weird.) Yet going a lifetime without participating in this "sport" is really kind of lame. You have to get your fantasy football on for at least one NFL season.

Chances are, you've been invited to join a league by friends or coworkers. Next time it comes up, just say yes. The rules will be understandable and the demands on your time reasonable. In a nutshell: You'll draft a roster of players (who doesn't want to play general manager for a day?), agonize over the order in which you select your offensive skill players (the fantasy points-scorers), and then have fun every week of the season as you cheer them on. You'll also experience following the league in a different way than ever before: It won't

Jrew	Jacobs	Slaton	Johnson	Jackson	Tomlinson	Gore	Moss	Johnson	White	Portis
:h	Gonzalez	Jones	Brown	Owens	White	Rivers	Colston	Smith	Wayne	Barber
n	Grant	Thomas	Warner	Romo	Jennings	Parker	Addai	Houshmandzadeh	McFadden	Welker
nt	Edwards	Williams	Jackson	Stewart	Jackson	Gonzalez	Clark	Bush	OCHO CINCO	Gates
es	Cooley	Berrian	Johnson	Ward	Rice	Brown	Wells	Schaub	Olsen	Ryan
ery	Royal	Holmes	Ravens	Daniels	Steelers	Coles	Jones	Moreno	Marshall	Benson
r	Titans	Jones	Shiancoe	Walter	Palmer	Giants	Mason	Lewis	Bears	Panthers
	Jackson	Cowboys	Avery	Taylor	Shockey	McCoy	Vikings	Chargers	Norwood	Moore
ow	Cutler	Carlson	Washington	Cassel	Bradshaw	Ginn Jr.	Hixon	Mendenhall	Roethlisberger	Hester
rd	Hightower	Harvin	Williams	Jets	Smith	Morgan	Gostkowski	Hasselbeck	Breaston	FAVRE
ain	Keller	Charles	Branch	Taylor	Bennett	Greene	Boss	Crabtree	Curtis	Betts
ng	Bironas	Pennington	Brown	Longwell	Miller	Campbell	Flacco	Scheffler	Graham	Coffee
ers	Muhammad	Buccaneers	Orton	Patriots	Delhomme	Crosby	Fargas	Crayton	Akers	Gage
ns	Washington	Vinatieri	Austin	Celek	Hartley	Scaife	Nicks	Gould	Fasano	Kasay
	15	15	15	15	15	15	15	15	15	15
ers	Manning	Brady	Bowe	Smith	Williams	Fitzgerald	Brees	Peterson	McNabb	Forte
7	17	17	17	17	17	17	17	17	17	17
	18	18	18	18	18	18	18	18	18	18
	19	19	19	19	19	19	19	19	19	19
	20	20	20	20	20	20	20	20	20	20

be about who wins and who loses, but about who hits pay dirt and who doesn't. Look, it's a blast. Your Week 5 matchup against Fred from accounting will be surprisingly thrilling.

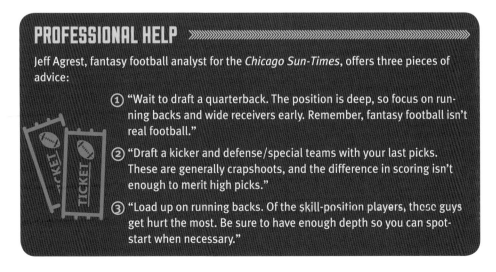

PROFESSIONAL HELP

Jeff Agrest, fantasy football analyst for the *Chicago Sun-Times*, offers three pieces of advice:

1. "Wait to draft a quarterback. The position is deep, so focus on running backs and wide receivers early. Remember, fantasy football isn't real football."

2. "Draft a kicker and defense/special teams with your last picks. These are generally crapshoots, and the difference in scoring isn't enough to merit high picks."

3. "Load up on running backs. Of the skill-position players, these guys get hurt the most. Be sure to have enough depth so you can spot-start when necessary."

DO THE PUNT, PASS & KICK

SOMEDAY THERE COULD BE—though probably not—a player who takes the NFL by storm as a punter, quarterback, and placekicker. The beauty of being young is believing that all things are possible. And even if they aren't, there's still the NFL-sponsored Punt, Pass & Kick competition. There are competition sites in every NFL market, and there's no charge to get in on the fun. Age groups break down thusly: 6/7, 8/9, 10/11, 12/13, and 14/15. With passing, both distance and accuracy are measured (simply, the ball must be thrown pretty straight). With punting and kicking, it's purely about distance. The kicking is done off tees; goalposts and crossbars are not involved. As for punting, leave the rugby style at the door—distance is measured strictly by where the ball makes initial contact with the ground.

The best competitors have to make it through a couple of rounds to advance to NFL team championships; from there, it's on to the national finals (for which Kansas 12-year-old Kendra Wecker, who later played in the WNBA, famously qualified in the boys' division

We've all got a little quarterback in us . . . and a little punter and kicker. (For some of us, very little.) Cheer on those girls and boys as they see how they measure up.

a couple of decades ago). By the way, who says it has to be an official deal for you to take your shot? There's no law forbidding a group of adults from gathering in a neighborhood park and staging their own comically unimpressive punt, pass, and kick competition.

PROFESSIONAL HELP

Sean Landeta, six-time NFL All-Pro punter and member of the league's 1980s and 1990s All-Decade teams, offers the following advice on punting: "The keys to punting a ball as high and far as possible are leg strength, leg speed, and hitting the ball pure. All punters know how important the quality of your drop—so your foot meets the ball in the exact right position to punt it squarely—is. Keep the laces straight up. You're trying to hit the exact middle of the bottom side of the football, where the ball is roundest, with the instep of your foot. And keep your toes pointed down, bent toward the ground, almost like a gymnast."

DO IT YOURSELF: THE COMBINE

YOU'RE FIT (or maybe not). You're ready (again, not). This is your calling to put yourself through the paces of the NFL Scouting Combine, the beef factory at which college football standouts are judged every February. We all know the 40-yard dash and the 225-pound bench press. Yet there are many other assessments, including the vertical- and broad-jump tests. There's the 20-yard shuttle: Put your hand in the dirt and run 5 yards up (touch the yard line), 10 yards back (touch it again), and 5 yards back to where you started from. There's the three-cone drill (look it up; it's too complicated to explain). There are many other physical drills, to say nothing of the mental ones—like the Wonderlic test, which can be taken online.

The point is, do it all. No, not because you're pondering a career change, but because you ought to see what these draft prospects go through before you judge them. If you can't push up 225 on the bench even once, then admire an oft-ridiculed quarterback like

>> It's possible—hey, we're just saying possible—your 40-yard dash time and vertical leap aren't NFL material. How will you know unless you give these drills a whirl? Next stop? Training Camp!

Jay Cutler, who heaved that weight more than 20 times, achieving one of the highest totals ever for a player at his position. And the really good news: You won't have to stand at the front of a crowded room in your underwear, as Combine invites long have done before an audience of the most critical judges in football.

PROFESSIONAL HELP >>>>>>>>>>>>>>>>>>>>>>

Matt Ryan, quarterback of the Atlanta Falcons, offers three pieces of advice:

① "Just try your hardest. It doesn't matter if the guy before you or the guy after you is faster or whatever—you're chasing your dream."

② "Work hard and be humble. That's my motto. But I'm not a great athlete. I'm more like a regular guy, I guess."

③ "This stuff is hard. I like playing football better."

>> Any youth football coaching staff would be lucky to add a newcomer who's in it purely for the benefit of the kids. It's a noble mentoring role that's been around a long time.

COACH A YOUTH FOOTBALL TEAM

AMERICAN PARTICIPATION in youth football has declined in recent years, due in part to safety concerns that exist at all levels, but more than 1.2 million youth ages 6–12 played organized tackle football in the United States in 2015, according to the Sports & Fitness Industry Association. (A similar number within that age group played flag football in 2015.) That's a whole lot of young boys (and girls) getting after it, maybe even one of yours. They need proper training. They need positive role models. They need pats on the helmet and, every now and then, a well-timed hug. Pop Warner leagues are open to players as young as five years old (and as strapping as 35 pounds). American Youth Football offers noncompetitive instructional leagues for children under 10; competitive leagues start with the 10U division.

Not everyone who coaches youth football must be an aspiring Vince Lombardi. Not everyone has to be a head coach, either. Every team needs a staff of coaches, all of them volunteers, to lead it, and the experience of coaching—and mentoring—children is just

plain priceless. If your child wants to play football, raise a hand and offer your services, too. If you don't have a football-playing child, raise a hand and do the same. But you will have to study up on both player safety and, you know, Xs and Os.

PROFESSIONAL HELP ≫≫≫≫≫≫≫≫≫≫≫≫≫≫≫≫≫≫≫≫≫≫≫≫≫≫≫

Tom Flores, head coach of the Super Bowl XV champion Oakland Raiders and the Super Bowl XVIII champion Los Angeles Raiders, offers three pieces of advice:

① "If you're going to coach young kids, my feeling is keep it simple, be well-organized, and be very patient."

② "These kids don't have long attention spans. They're going to make mistakes. They're going to drive you crazy. But you have to make it fun for them."

③ "It doesn't matter what's the age—discipline is very good."

CHAPTER 8

I LOVE L.A.

THE LATE Elizabeth Taylor once said, "Marriage is a great institution." Something tells us a starlet who was married eight times would've been OK with the city's latest tying of the knot with the NFL. Many others are skeptical. Los Angeles again has the Rams, who played there from 1946 to 1979, moved to Anaheim in 1980 and to St. Louis in 1995, and then returned to L.A. for the 2016 season. The Raiders gave L.A. a go from 1982 to 1994 before returning to Oakland. The city never worked for the Los Angeles Express of the erstwhile United States Football League, who ranked at the bottom of that league in attendance. There are kneejerk explanations for all of this—too much else to do here, too many transplants who root for their childhood teams.

Yet here the Rams are—playing temporarily at the Los Angeles Memorial Coliseum—with the San Diego Chargers planning to join them at City of Champions Stadium for a spectacular 2019 opening season. Being built to host two NFL teams, City of Champions Stadium is the grandest building project in American football history. It is under construction in Inglewood, with a price tag of $2.5 billion.

Expected to be the most expensive sports venue in the world, the wave-shaped stadium complex—set 100 feet into the ground—will include a 6,000-seat concert venue housed under the same futuristic, sail-shaped transparent roof. Surrounding the complex will be the rest of the Los Angeles Stadium and Entertainment District at Hollywood Park—vast swaths of retail space (including many restaurants and bars), a luxury hotel, green space, a lake, transit access, and more. The Super Bowl will be here in February of 2021. Road trip to end all road trips?

≫ Los Angeles still must prove
to doubters that it can be a
great football market. One
thing is certain, though: Its
new stadium complex will be a
wonder of the sporting world.

» May the stands remain filled with screaming fans.

A DIRECTORY OF FOOTBALL DESTINATIONS

NEW ENGLAND

Gillette Stadium
1 Patriot Pl.
Foxborough, MA 02035
- In chapter 6, *Rites of Passage* (End Zone Militia)

Harvard Stadium
79 N. Harvard St.
Allston, MA 02134
- In chapter 2, *Bad Blood* (College Football Rivalries: Harvard vs. Yale)

Yale Bowl
81 Central Ave.
New Haven, CT 06515
- In chapters 2, *Bad Blood* (College Football Rivalries: Harvard vs. Yale); and 3, *No Place Like Home* (Sightseeing: Walter Camp Gate)

MID-ATLANTIC

Beaver Stadium
1 Beaver Stadium
University Park, PA
- In chapter 3, *No Place Like Home* (Eight Hundred Club)

>> The Auburn Tigers charge into Jordan-Hare Stadium, 2010

Bergen Catholic High School
1040 Oradell Ave.
Oradell, NJ 07649
- In chapter 2, *Bad Blood* (High School Rivalries: Don Bosco Prep vs. Bergen Catholic)

Don Bosco Preparatory High School
492 Franklin Turnpike
Ramsey, NJ 07446
- In chapter 2, *Bad Blood* (High School Rivalries: Don Bosco Prep vs. Bergen Catholic)

FedEx Field
1600 FedEx Way
Hyattsville, MD 20785
- In chapters 1, *Meccas and Museums* (Must-See Museums: NFL Rings of Honor); and 2, *Bad Blood* (NFL Rivalries: Cowboys vs. Redskins)

Fisher Stadium
218 A P Kirby Sports Ctr.
Easton, PA 18042
- In chapter 2, *Bad Blood* (College Football Rivalries: Lafayette vs. Lehigh)

Goodman Stadium
150 Goodman Ctr.
Bethlehem, PA 18015
- In chapter 2, *Bad Blood* (College Football Rivalries: Lafayette vs. Lehigh)

Heinz Field
100 Art Rooney Ave.
Pittsburgh, PA 15212
- In chapters 2, *Bad Blood* (NFL Rivalries: Ravens vs. Steelers); 4, *Seats . . . and Eats* (Eats: Primanti Bros.); and 6, *Rites of Passage* (Terrible Towels)

》 The University of Alabama's marching band

Lincoln Financial Field
1 Lincoln Financial Field Way
Philadelphia, PA 19148
- In chapter 2, *Bad Blood* (NFL Rivalries: Eagles vs. Giants, College Football Rivalries: Army vs. Navy)

M&T Bank Stadium
1101 Russell St.
Baltimore, MD 21230
- In chapters 1, *Meccas and Museums* (Must-See Museums: NFL Rings of Honor); 2, *Bad Blood* (NFL Rivalries: Ravens vs. Steelers); and 5, *Tailgating . . . and Sailgating*

MetLife Stadium
1 MetLife Stadium Dr.
East Rutherford, NJ 07073
- In chapters 1, *Meccas and Museums* (Must-See Museums: NFL Rings of Honor); 2, *Bad Blood* (NFL Rivalries: Eagles vs. Giants); and 4, *Seats . . . and Eats* (Eats: Kitchen Sink)

Michie Stadium
United States Military Academy
700 Mille Rd.
West Point, NY 10996
- In chapter 3, *No Place Like Home* (One-of-a-Kind)

New Era Field
1 Bills Dr.
Orchard Park, NY 14127
- In chapters 1, *Meccas and Museums* (Must-See Museums: NFL Rings of Honor); 5, and *Tailgating . . . and Sailgating*

THE SOUTH

Bobby Dodd Stadium
North Avenue NW
Atlanta, GA 30313
- In chapter 2, *Bad Blood* (College Football Rivalries: Georgia vs. Georgia Tech)

Bryant-Denny Stadium
920 Paul W Bryant Dr.
Tuscaloosa, AL 35401

» The 1891 Rutgers football team

- In chapters 2, *Bad Blood* (College Football Rivalries: Alabama vs. Auburn); and 3, *No Place Like Home* (Eight Hundred Club)

Camping World Stadium
1 Citrus Bowl Pl.
Orlando, FL 32805
- In chapters 2, *Bad Blood* (College Football Rivalries: Bethune-Cookman vs. Florida A&M); and 7, *Just Do It* (Go to the Pro Bowl)

College Football Hall of Fame
250 Marietta St NW
Atlanta, GA 30313
- In chapter 1, *Meccas and Museums* (Must-See Museums)

Davis Wade Stadium
90 B. S. Hood Rd.
Mississippi State University, MS 39762
- In chapter 2, *Bad Blood* (College Football Rivalries: Ole Miss vs. Mississippi State)

Donald W. Reynolds Razorback Stadium
350 N Razorback Rd.
Fayetteville, AR 72701
- In chapters 2, *Bad Blood* (College Football Rivalries: Arkansas vs. LSU); and 6, *Rites of Passage* (Calling the Hogs)

EverBank Field
1 EverBank Field Dr.
Jacksonville, FL 32202
- In chapters 2, *Bad Blood* (College Football Rivalries: Florida vs. Georgia); and 4, *Seats . . . and Eats* (Fanduelville)

Hard Rock Stadium
347 Don Shula Dr.
Miami Gardens, FL 33056
In chapter 1, *Meccas and Museums* (Must-See Museums: NFL Rings of Honor)

Jordan-Hare Stadium
Auburn University
251 S Donahue Dr.
Auburn, AL 36849
- In chapters 2, *Bad Blood* (College Football Rivalries: Alabama vs. Auburn); and 6, *Rites of Passage* (Rolling of Toomer's Corner)

Legion Field
400 Graymont Ave.
Birmingham, AL 35205
- In chapter 2, *Bad Blood* (College Football Rivalries: Alabama State vs. Alabama A&M)

Male High School
4409 Preston Hwy.
Louisville, KY 40213
- In chapter 2, *Bad Blood* (High School Rivalries: Male vs. Manual)

Memorial Stadium
Clemson University
1 Avenue of Champions
Clemson, SC 29634
- In chapters 2, *Bad Blood* (College Football Rivalries: Clemson vs. South Carolina); and 6, *Rites of Passage* (Rubbing Howard's Rock)

Mercedes-Benz Superdome
1500 Sugar Bowl Dr.
New Orleans, LA 70112
- In chapters 1, *Meccas and Museums*; and 2, *Bad Blood* (College Football Rivalries: Grambling vs. Southern)

Neyland Stadium
1235 Phillip Fulmer Way
Knoxville, TN 37916
- In chapters 3, *No Place Like Home* (Eight Hundred Club); and 5, *Tailgating . . . and Sailgating*

Raymond James Stadium
4201 N Dale Mabry Hwy.
Tampa, FL 33607
- In chapter 3, *No Place Like Home* (Sightseeing: Pirate Ship)

Sanford Stadium
100 Sanford Dr.
Athens, GA 30602
- In chapter 2, *Bad Blood* (College Football Rivalries: Georgia vs. Georgia Tech)

Tiger Stadium
Louisiana State University
Baton Rouge, LA 70803
- In chapters 2, *Bad Blood* (College Football Rivalries: Arkansas vs. LSU); and 3, *No Place Like Home* (Eight Hundred Club)

Vaught-Hemingway Stadium
All-America Dr & Hill Dr.
University, MS 38677

- In chapters 2, *Bad Blood* (College Football Rivalries: Ole Miss vs. Mississippi State); and 5, *Tailgating . . . and Sailgating* (The Grove)

Williams-Brice Stadium
1125 George Rogers Blvd.
Columbia, SC 29201

- In chapters 2, *Bad Blood* (College Football Rivalries: Clemson vs. South Carolina); and 5, *Tailgating . . . and Sailgating* (Cockabooses)

THE MIDWEST

Arrowhead Stadium
1 Arrowhead Dr.
Kansas City, MO 64129

- In chapters 1, *Meccas and Museums* (Must-See Museums: NFL Rings of Honor); and 5, *Tailgating . . . and Sailgating*

Camp Randall Stadium
1440 Monroe St.
Madison, WI 53711

- In chapters 2, *Bad Blood* (College Football Rivalries: Minnesota vs. Wisconsin); 5, *Tailgating . . . and Sailgating* (House Parties); and 6, *Rites of Passage* ("Jump Around")

Fargodome
1800 N University Dr.
Fargo, ND 58102

- In chapter 3, *No Place Like Home* (One-of-a-Kind)

Fawcett Stadium
1815 Harrison Ave NW
Canton, OH 44708

- In chapter 2, *Bad Blood* (High School Rivalries: Canton McKinley vs. Massillon Washington)

FirstEnergy Stadium
100 Alfred Lerner Way
Cleveland, OH 44114

- In chapters 4, *Seats . . . and Eats* (Seats: Dawg Pound); and 5, *Tailgating . . . and Sailgating*

Lambeau Field
1265 Lombardi Ave
Green Bay, WI 54304

- In chapters 1, *Meccas and Museums, Bad Blood* (NFL Rivalries: Bears vs. Packers); and 4, *Seats . . . and Eats* (Seats: Lambeau Leap Zone)

Lucas Oil Stadium
500 S Capitol Ave.
Indianapolis, IN 46225

- In chapter 4, *Seats . . . and Eats* (Eats: Jumbo Pork Tenderloin)

Michigan Stadium
1201 S Main St.
Ann Arbor, MI 48104

- In chapters 2, *Bad Blood* (College Football Rivalries: Michigan vs. Ohio State); and 3, *No Place Like Home* (Eight Hundred Club)

Notre Dame Stadium
University of Notre Dame
Moose Krause Cir.
Notre Dame, IN 46556

- In chapters 1, *Meccas and Museums*, and 2, *Bad Blood* (College Football Rivalries: Notre Dame vs. USC)

Ohio Stadium
The Ohio State University
411 Woody Hayes Dr.
Columbus, OH 43210

- In chapters 2, *Bad Blood* (College Football Rivalries: Michigan vs. Ohio State); and 3, *No Place Like Home* (Eight Hundred Club)

Pro Football Hall of Fame
2121 George Halas Dr. NW
Canton, OH 44708

- In chapter 1, *Meccas and Museums*

Soldier Field
1410 Museum Campus Dr.
Chicago, IL 60605

- In chapters 1, *Meccas and Museums*, and 2, *Bad Blood* (NFL Rivalries: Bears vs. Packers)

TCF Bank Stadium
420 SE 23rd Ave.
Minneapolis, MN 55455

- In chapter 2, *Bad Blood* (College Football Rivalries: Minnesota vs. Wisconsin)

U.S. Bank Stadium
401 Chicago Ave.
Minneapolis, MN 55415

- In chapter 3, *No Place Like Home* (One-of-a-Kind)

Washington High School
1 Paul E. Brown Dr. SE
Massillon, OH 44646

- In chapter 2, *Bad Blood* (High School Rivalries: Canton McKinley vs. Massillon Washington)

THE SOUTHWEST

AT&T Stadium
1 AT&T Way
Arlington, TX 76011

- In chapters 1, *Meccas and Museums* (Must-See Museums: NFL Rings of Honor); 2, *Bad Blood* (NFL Rivalries: Cowboys vs. Redskins); 3, *No Place Like Home* (Sightseeing: Scoreboard at AT&T Stadium); and 4, *Seats . . . and Eats* (Eats: Texas Torta)

Boone Pickens Stadium
700 W. Hall of Fame Ave.
Stillwater, OK 74075

- In chapter 2, *Bad Blood* (College Football Rivalries: Oklahoma vs. Oklahoma State)

Cotton Bowl Stadium
3750 The Midway
Dallas, TX 75215

- In chapter 2, *Bad Blood* (College Football Rivalries: Oklahoma vs. Texas)

Eagle Stadium
155 Rivercrest Blvd.
Allen, TX 75002

- In chapter 3, *No Place Like Home* (One-of-a-Kind)

Kyle Field
Texas A&M University
757 Houston St.
College Station, TX 77843

- In chapter 3, *No Place Like Home* (Eight Hundred Club)

McLane Stadium
1001 S. MLK Jr. Blvd.
Waco, TX 76704

- In chapter 3, *No Place Like Home* (One-of-a-Kind)

》 Football players in Minot, North Dakota, 1940

Monument Valley High School
100 Cougar Ln.
Oljato-Monument Valley, UT 84536
• In chapter 3, *No Place Like Home* (One-of-a-Kind)

NRG Stadium
NRG Pkwy.
Houston, TX 77054
• In chapter 5, *Tailgating . . . and Sailgating*

Oklahoma Memorial Stadium
1185 Asp Ave.
Norman, OK 73019
• In chapter 2, *Bad Blood* (College Football Rivalries: Oklahoma vs. Oklahoma State)

Ratliff Stadium
1862 E. Yukon Rd.
Odessa, TX 79765
• In chapter 1, *Meccas and Museums*

Skelly Field
3112 E 8th St.
Tulsa, OK 7414
• In chapter 2, *Bad Blood* (High School Rivalries: Jenks vs. Union)

Texas Memorial Stadium
405 E 23rd St.
Austin, TX 78712
• In chapter 3, *No Place Like Home* (Eight Hundred Club)

THE WEST

Albertsons Stadium
1400 Bronco Ln.
Boise, ID 83706
• In chapter 3, *No Place Like Home* (Sightseeing: Blue Turf)

Aloha Stadium
99-500 Salt Lake Blvd.
Aiea, HI 96818
• In chapter 6, *Rites of Passage* (The Haka)

Angel Stadium of Anaheim
2000 E. Gene Autry Way
Anaheim, CA 92806
• In chapter 2, *Bad Blood* (High School Rivalries: Mater Dei vs. Servite)

Autzen Stadium
2700 MLK Jr. Blvd.
Eugene, OR 97401
• In chapter 2, *Bad Blood* (College Football Rivalries: Oregon vs. Oregon State)

Caesars Palace
3570 S. Las Vegas Blvd.
Las Vegas, NV 89109
• In chapter 7, *Just Do It* (Spend a Weekend in a Las Vegas Sports Book)

California Memorial Stadium
2227 Piedmont Ave.
Berkeley, CA 94720
• In chapter 2, *Bad Blood* (College Football Rivalries: Cal vs. Stanford)

CenturyLink Field
800 Occidental Ave. S
Seattle, WA 98134
• In chapters 4, *Seats . . . and Eats* (Seats: Hawks Nest); and 6, *Rites of Passage* (12th Man Flags)

Los Angeles Stadium
Hollywood Park
Inglewood, CA 90301
• In chapter 8, *I Love L.A.*

Folson Field
2400 Colorado Ave.
Boulder, CO 80302
• In chapter 6, *Rites of Passage* (Ralphie's Run)

Husky Stadium
3800 Montlake Blvd. NE
Seattle, WA 98195
• In chapter 5, *Tailgating . . . and Sailgating*

Lavell Edwards Stadium
1700 N. Canyon Rd.
Provo, UT 84604
• In chapter 2, *Bad Blood* (College Football Rivalries: BYU vs. Utah)

Los Angeles Memorial Coliseum
3911 S. Figueroa St.
Los Angeles, CA 90037
• In chapter 2, *Bad Blood* (College Football Rivalries: Notre Dame vs. USC)

Oakland Coliseum
7000 Coliseum Way
Oakland, CA 94621
- In chapters 2, *Bad Blood* (NFL Rivalries: Broncos vs. Raiders); and 4, *Seats . . . and Eats* (Seats: Black Hole)

Reser Stadium
660 SW 26th St.
Corvallis, OR 97331
- In chapter 2, *Bad Blood* (College Football Rivalries: Oregon vs. Oregon State)

Rice-Eccles Stadium
The University of Utah
451 1400 E
Salt Lake City, UT 84112
- In chapter 2, *Bad Blood* (College Football Rivalries: BYU vs. Utah)

Roos Field
1136 Washington St.
Cheney, WA 99004
- In chapter 3, *No Place Like Home* (Sightseeing: Red Turf)

Rose Bowl Stadium
1001 Rose Bowl Dr.
Pasadena, CA 91103
- In chapters 1, *Meccas and Museums*, and 6, *Rites of Passage* (The Rose Parade)

Sports Authority Field at Mile High
1701 Bryant St.
Denver, CO 80204
- In chapter 2, *Bad Blood* (NFL Rivalries: Broncos vs. Raiders)

Stadium Bowl
111 N E St.
Tacoma, WA 98498
- In chapter 3, *No Place Like Home* (One-of-a-Kind)

Stanford Stadium
Stanford University
625 Nelson Rd.
Stanford, CA 94305
- In chapter 2, *Bad Blood* (College Football Rivalries: Cal vs. Stanford)

University of Phoenix Stadium
1 Cardinals Dr.
Glendale, AZ 85305
- In chapter 4, *Seats . . . and Eats* (Eats: Pizza Box Nachos)

CANADA

Tim Hortons Field
64 Melrose Ave. N
Hamilton, ON L8L 8C1
- In chapter 2, *Meccas and Museums* (Must-See Museums: Canadian Football League Hall of Fame)

》 Football legend Jim Thorpe

ACKNOWLEDGMENTS

I am indebted to Keith Wallman of Lyons Press for his amiable guidance and patience, and to Albert Dickson for his keen eye and many years of friendship. Thank you to Mike DeCourcy for introducing me to Lyons Press. Thanks especially to Chris De Luca, my editor at the *Chicago Sun-Times*, for his hands-off approach when buckling down on this project was necessary.

Thanks to the many coaches and players—some of them retired—who took time to help, and to the behind-the-scenes people who provided needed information and

context. Thanks to friends in the business (and not) who offered support: Matt Hayes, Matt Crossman, Scott Campbell, Gordon Wittenmyer, Phil Wagner, Dick Liberman, Norby Langendorf.

Thanks to John Rawlings for hiring me many years ago at the *Sporting News*, and to Jeff D'Alessio for encouraging my move from editor to writer. And thanks to my SN family—Tom Dienhart, Ken Bradley, Bob Hille, Dale Bye, Mike Nahrstedt, Corrie Anderson-Gifford, and many others—for such wonderful, formative years.

And thank you, especially, to my parents and my wife for their endless reassurance.

» Army vs. Navy at the Polo Grounds in New York City, 1916.

INDEX

Dallas Cowboys Cheerleader, 2014

》Football in the 1920s

>> Cheerleading for the University of Alabama

》Exeter vs. Andover, a high-school rivalry
nearly 150 years old

≫ Old school youth football

» Ye olde tackling dummy, Harvard, 1912

>> California-Stanford game in Berkeley, California, 1930

» Four muddy Navy players, 1945

» Fans at Duke–North Carolina game, 1939

» Slingin' Sammy Baugh in 1937

》Chicago Bears teammates Joe Zeller and Red Grange, 1935

PHOTO CREDITS

ii   Frontispiece photo: Courtesy of Texas A&M

vi   Photo opposite contents: AP Photo/Elise Amendola

viii   Chapter III inset in contents—By Andrew Horne—Own work, CC BY 3.0, https://commons.wikimedia.org/w/index.php?curid=12109066

x   College football diehards from 1957: Courtesy of the Library of Congress (also on pp. 226–27)

xxi, 1   Introduction photos: Leprechaun—Icon Sportswire via AP Images; panorama at Michigan—By Andrew Horne—Own work, CC BY 3.0, https://commons.wikimedia.org/w/index.php?curid=12109066; Marcus Mariota running with ball—GoDucks.com

Chapter I. Meccas and Museums

2, 3   Chapter opener photos: Outside Lambeau Field—AP Photo/Scott Boehm; Notre Dame Stadium interior—Scott Boehm via AP

Football Meccas

4, 5   Lambeau Field: Statue outside stadium—AP Photo/David Stluka; stadium fireworks—Scott Boehm via AP (also on p. vii)

6   Soldier Field—Scott Boehm via AP

8   Mercedes-Benz Superdome—By Daniel Schwen—Own work, CC BY-SA 4.0, https://commons.wikimedia.org/w/index.php?curid=7081892

10, 11   Notre Dame Stadium: Leprechaun—Photo by Robin Alam, Icon Sportswire via AP Images; stadium and Touchdown Jesus—Icon Sportswire via AP Images

12   Rose Bowl Stadium—By Flickr user Xurble—Flickr, CC BY 2.0, https://commons.wikimedia.org/w/index.php?curid=1651593

13   Rose Bowl Stadium: Rose Bowl 2014 at dusk by Andy Walker, CC BY-ND 2.0, https://www.flickr.com/photos/awalker/16137805367/sizes/l

14, 15   Ratliff Stadium—AP Photo/Odessa American, Edyta Blaszczyk; By Zorino9—Taken by self, CC BY 3.0, https://commons.wikimedia.org/w/index.php?curid=14607622

Must-See Museums

16   Pro Football Hall of Fame—AP Photo/Aaron M. Sprecher

18, 19   College Football Hall of Fame—Both photos Courtesy of the College Football Hall of Fame

20, 21   Canadian Football League Hall of Fame: Busts—*Canadian Press*/John Woods; Grey Cup 1960—Vancouver Public Library

22 NFL Rings of Honor—By www.flickr.com/photos/sidurkin—www.flickr.com/photos/sidurkin/2051015759/in/set-72157603250445022, CC BY-SA 2.0, https://commons.wikimedia.org/w/index.php?curid=6906660

23 NFL Rings of Honor—"Jim Brown" by Erik Drost, https://www.flickr.com/photos/edrost88/6856222285/sizes/l , CC BY 2.0

24 In Honor of Meccas Lost to History (Miami Orange Bowl)—Original uploader was Haaron755 at English Wikipedia; transferred from en.wikipedia to Commons, CC BY-SA 3.0, https://commons.wikipedia.org/w/index.php?curid=2507084

25 In Honor of Meccas Lost to History: Candlestick Park—Photographs in the Carol M. Highsmith Archive, Library of Congress, Prints and Photographs Division

Chapter II. Bad Blood

26, 27 Chapter opener photo—Icon Sportswire via AP Images

NFL Rivalries

28 Bears vs. Packers—AP Photo/Jeff Roberson

29 Bears vs. Packers—By Paul Cutler from Chaska, USA - IMG_0954.JPG, CC BY-SA 2.0, https://commons.wikimedia.org/w/index.php?curid=3441226

30, 31 Cowboys vs. Redskins: Staubach scrambles—AP Photo/NFL Photos; Staubach is hit—Photo by Arnie Sachs/picture-alliance/dpa/AP Images

32 Broncos vs. Raiders—NFL Contributor via AP Images

33 Broncos vs. Raiders—AP Photo/Kevork Djansezian

34 Eagles vs. Giants—Al Tielemans via AP Images

36 Ravens vs. Steelers—AP Photo/Tom E. Puskar

37 Ravens vs. Steelers—AP Photo/Patrick Semansky

College Football Rivalries

   Dirty Dozen: Major College Home-and-Homes

38, 39 The Game: Michigan vs. Ohio State: Bo Schembechler and Woody Hayes—AP Photo/File; Buckeye celebration—Icon Sportswire via AP Images

40 Iron Bowl: Alabama vs. Auburn—Courtesy of Auburn Athletics

41 Iron Bowl: Alabama vs. Auburn—By Matthew Tosh—originally posted to Flickr as DSCF1613, CC BY-SA 2.0, https://commons.wikimedia.org/w/index.php?curid=12350899

High School Rivalries

74, 75   Mater Dei vs. Servite, red and white helmet vs. black helmet—Courtesy of Frank Losoya/Mater
          Dei High School; Male vs. Manual (Louisville), gold helmet vs. red helmets—Courtesy of Rich
          Bowling/Male; Canton McKinley vs. Massillon, white helmets vs. black and orange helmets—
          Courtesy of CantonRep.com/Bob Rossiter; Jenks vs. Union, trophy—AP Photo/*Tulsa World*,
          Stephan Holman

Chapter III. No Place Like Home

76, 77   Chapter opener photos: Neyland Stadium interior—Icon Sportswire via AP Images; McLane
          Stadium—Courtesy of Baylor University Marketing & Communications

The Eight Hundred Club: Over 100,000 Capacity. Only in College Football.

78   The Big House (Michigan)—By Andrew Horne—Own work, CC BY-SA 3.0, https://commons
          .wikimedia.org/w/index.php?curid=16542210

80   Beaver Stadium (Penn State)—By Acroterion—Own work, CC BY-SA 3.0, https://commons
          .wikimedia.org/w/index.php?curid=3455574

81   Beaver Stadium (Penn State)—By Batistaya—Own work, Public Domain, https://commons
          .wikimedia.org/w/index.php?curid=5914843

82, 83   Ohio Stadium (Ohio State): Panorama—By Lil Nors—Own work, CC BY-SA 4.0, https://commons
          .wikimedia.org/w/index.php?curid=47878793; exterior corner—By Ibagli—Own work, Public
          Domain, https://commons.wikimedia.org/w/index.php?curid=6667591

84   Kyle Field (Texas A&M)—Courtesy of Texas A&M

86   Neyland Stadium (Tennessee)—AP Photo/Wade Payne

88   Tiger Stadium (LSU)—Steve Franz/LSU Athletics

89   Tiger Stadium (LSU): photo of tiger statue—"DSC00156-1" by getmahesh, https://www.flickr
          .com/photos/getmahesh/8245144684/sizes/l, CC BY-SA 2.0

90   Bryant-Denny Stadium (Alabama)—AP Photo/Butch Dill

92, 93   Darrell K. Royal Memorial Stadium (Texas): Texas flag on field—By Klobetime—DSC02314,
          CC BY-SA 2.0, https://commons.wikimedia.org/w/index.php?curid=3291290; panorama—By
          Dave Wilson from Austin, Texas, USA—UT/Rice Football Game Panorama, CC BY-SA 2.0, https://
          commons.wikimedia.org/w/index.php?curid=2818025

One-of-a-Kind

94   U.S. Bank Stadium (Minnesota Vikings)—By Darbo2—Own work, CC BY-SA 4.0, https://
          commons.wikimedia.org/w/index.php?curid=50320917

95   US Bank Stadium (Minnesota Vikings)—By Darbo2 - Own work, CC BY-SA 4.0, https://
          commons.wikimedia.org/w/index.php?curid=50321059

Chapter IV. Seats . . . and Eats

Chapter VIII. I Love L.A.

A Directory of Football Destinations

Acknowledgments

Index

Photo Credits

About the Author

≫ Going to a Yale-Princeton game, 1910

≫ Michigan Stadium, 2015

ABOUT THE AUTHOR

Steve Greenberg has written for the *Chicago Sun-Times*, the *New York Times*, the *Sporting News*, *Inside Sports*, and *Basketball News*. He has covered dozens of postseasons in college football, college basketball, the NFL, the NBA, the NHL, and Major League Baseball. Currently the national college and Cubs columnist for the *Chicago Sun-Times*, from 2011 to 2013 he was a college football writer for the *Sporting News*. He has also worked for *Football Digest* and *Hockey Digest*, as well as being an on-air member of *Inside Sports*' national radio show. He lives in St. Louis with his wife and three children.

≫ Trumpets from the Wisconsin marching band, 2013

≫ Entrance at Soldier Field, Chicago